Special Needs in the Early Years

This book celebrates good practice in the area of early years and special needs by bringing together authors who are practitioners or researchers from a range of different and diverse early-years settings including nurseries and units providing special provision. They describe their work with young children who have different and distinctive special needs and disabilities.

The profile of special needs in the early years has risen recently as a consequence of government legislation; this has made increased provision for pupils with special needs a priority for education authorities and other early-years providers and has encouraged early-years practitioners to extend their skills. The authors of this book have extensive experience in working directly with young children and topics covered include:

- play activities
- working with children in a hospital setting
- integrating a child with Down's Syndrome
- working with children with hearing impediments
- behaviour management approaches in the early years
- assessment
- working with parents

The book will be relevant to early-years practitioners, researchers, policy makers, advisers, inspectors and educational psychologists.

Sheila Wolfendale has been a teacher as well as an educational psychologist. She is currently Professor and Director of the MSc and Doctorate educational psychology programmes at the University of East London.

Special Needs in the Early Years

Snapshots of practice

Edited by Sheila Wolfendale

London and New York

Charity Reg. No. 288955R

OMEP

First published 2000
by RoutledgeFalmer
2 Park Square, Milton Park,
Abingdon, Oxon, OX14 4RN

Simultaneously published in the USA and Canada
by RoutledgeFalmer
270 Madison Ave, New York NY 10016

RoutledgeFalmer is an imprint of the Taylor & Francis Group

Transferred to Digital Printing 2004

Typeset in Goudy by
Keystroke, Jacaranda Lodge, Wolverhampton

British Library Cataloguing in Publication Data
A catalogue record for this book is available
from the British Library

Library of Congress Cataloging in Publication Data
Special needs in the early years: snapshots of practice / edited by
  Sheila Wolfendale.
      p.   cm.
    Includes bibliographical references and index.
    1. Handicapped children—Education (Preschool)—Great Britain.
  2. Special education—Great Britain. I. Wolfendale, Sheila, 1939– .
  LC4036.G7S69   2000
  371.9'0472—dc21   99-44835
                                                  CIP

ISBN 0–415–21388–6 (hbk)
ISBN 0–415–21389–4 (pbk)

Contents

Figures

Contributors

Pamela Barnes is a nursery teacher, with a particular interest in children with special needs. She is a founder member of Action for Sick Children, formerly National Association of Welfare of Children in Hospital. Pamela set up the first Hospital Play programme in the North West in 1971 and was involved in this work for 20 years whilst Chairman of the National Association of Hospital Play Staff. She also set up the Hospital Play Staff Education Trust (HPSET) which is the academic board responsible for the training, qualification and registration of Hospital Play Specialists. She is currently HPS Tutor in Bolton, Greater Manchester, Non-Executive Director of Manchester Children's Trust and OMEP UK President.

Dr Tony Bertram is a Senior Research Fellow, Co-Director of the Centre for Research in Early Childhood at University College Worcester and President of the European Early Childhood Education Research Association. He taught in first and primary schools prior to working in higher education. His research interests include early childhood teacher training, admission of children to school, and men in early childhood.

Moira Evans is an experienced early-years teacher who has worked in nursery and infant classes in Sheffield and London. She has been involved in home visiting and support work in schools. She is presently the curriculum co-ordinator and is responsible for curriculum development and some inservice training in an Under Fives' Education Centre in London.

Jo Fieldhouse is an early years teacher who has worked with nursery children in Leicester. She is presently working as a PhD Research Student at the Centre for Research in Early Childhood at the University College Worcester. She is working with the Effective Early Learning Research Team to adapt the Effective Early Learning Project which is a new development and improvement strategy focused upon working with young children with special educational needs and their parents.

Sheila Gatiss trained as a paediatric nurse, with a postgraduate diploma in health education. She has served as a County Councillor, a member of a Regional

Health Authority and worked at the University of Cambridge, London School of Economics and the National Children's Bureau. Her campaigning career started with ensuring parents could visit and stay with their sick children whilst in hospital.

Fleur Griffiths was co-opted to teach special needs on the new Early Childhood Studies degree at the Sunderland University School of Education in September 1996. She started her career as a primary school teacher, and soon focussed on children with special educational needs. She became an educational psychologist and practised for 15 years, taking particular responsibility for language units. She continues to work with parents in partnership on the pre-school project for children with communication difficulties.

Joy Jarvis is a Senior Lecturer, currently responsible for the Post Graduate Diploma/Certificate in the Education of the Hearing-Impaired, at the University of Hertfordshire. She is a teacher of the deaf and has worked in a range of settings with deaf children and their families.

Moira Keating is a freelance Education Consultant and Trainer. She has worked with children and young people from ages 0–16. She was a Special Needs Advisory Teacher with the Inner London Education Authority and was in the primary inspectorate team in another Local Authority, where she was responsible for recruiting and designing the induction programme for newly qualified teachers. She was Head of an Under Fives' Education Centre in London and is an Ofsted Registered Nursery Inspector and NVQ Assessor. She is currently working with Local Authorities on the writing and implementation of their Early Years and Childcare Development Plans.

Elizabeth Knight has experience of working with under fives in social services and education settings. She has worked in London as an Under Fives' Development Officer which involved liaison with parents, childminders, play groups, community, council and private nurseries. She is an Ofsted Registered Nursery Inspector and has been the Deputy and SENCO in an Under Fives' Education Centre where she had responsibility for training staff on the implementation of the Code of Practice and Special Educational Needs.

Dr Andrew Lockett is the Early Years Inspector for Kirklees Local Education Authority. He completed his doctorate in the assessment of learning of 3–5 year olds with special educational needs. He has worked in a wide range of private, voluntary and maintained early-years settings. He has a particular interest in children from the Indian sub-continent following a period of teaching in the Himalaya mountains of North India. He enjoys sharing with young children his love of stories through storytelling using a range of media.

Dr Wendy Lynas is a Senior Lecturer in Education of the Deaf in the Centre for Human Communication and Deafness, University of Manchester. Her major academic interests and publications relate to communication options in the education of deaf children; the inclusion of deaf pupils in mainstream education; deaf children from minority ethnic groups. She is currently doing research on support for deaf pupils in mainstream schools, funded by the Teacher Training Agency, and 'good practice' in the education of deaf children, funded by RNID.

Dr Theodora Papatheodorou is a Senior Lecturer in SEN in the Canterbury Christ Church University College. She has a long and diverse teaching experience of working with young children in early years, special educational needs and bilingual settings. Her current research interests and activities refer to the use of stories and their relevance to affective development of young children, especially those children who have diverse needs, that is, children with special needs and children from cultural minorities. Community education for bilingual children and their families is also among her personal and professional interests.

Professor Christine Pascal holds the Chair in Early Childhood Education at University College Worcester. She is Co-Director of the Centre for Research in Early Childhhod and Vice-President of the British Association of Early Childhood Education. She taught in infant schools in Birmingham, and was a member of the RSA Start Right Inquiry into Early Learning. She is co-founder of the European Early Childhood Education Research Association and has worked with the association at the local, national, and international level to raise the status and quality of education for young children.

Helen Penn is Professor of Early Childhood at the University of East London. She has had a career in the voluntary and education sectors, including a period as Assistant Director of Education in Strathclyde when she was responsible for introducing the first integrated early-years department in the UK Since becoming an academic she has undertaken a series of research projects into different aspects of early-years education, in the UK and abroad. She also acts as consultant to Save the Children Fund, and has evaluated projects for them in Southern Africa and in a number of transitional (ex-communist) countries. Her publications include *Transforming Nursery Education* (with Peter Moss); and *Comparing Nurseries* a comparative study of day nurseries in Spain, Italy and the UK.

Karen Riley is a parent of a hearing daughter and a deaf son. She is a founder member of 'Listen Hear', a local support group for deaf children and their families, and is particularly interested in working with professionals and other parents to support families with deaf children. She is currently undertaking a post graduate course in the education of the hearing-impaired at the University of Hertfordshire.

Pamela Stanier has been Headteacher at Rodney House School since 1989. Her teaching career has followed her changing educational interests: first teaching

English (her degree subject) in a girls' grammar school and a comprehensive school; then work with children in the early years to pursue a growing interest in developmental psychology, and subsequently an interest in children with special needs whose development is not following a usual pattern. Her current professional interests are school management and developing new ways of working with parents.

Dr Susan Turner retired from her work as a teacher of the deaf with responsibility for deaf children under five and their families in 1989. She has since worked in the Centre for Human Communication and Deafness, University of Manchester as an honorary tutor working with distance learning students. Her research interests focus on the needs of pre-school deaf children in families of ethnic minority origin.

Sylvia Walker Sylvia is the Principal Training & Development Officer for Sheffield LEA support staff and has worked in the Training Section for 10 years. Prior to becoming a Training Officer she worked as a Nursery Nurse, and now works primarily with support staff in schools, identifying training needs, planning training, ensuring quality. She has been a member, Chair and Co-ordinator of SECA for over 20 years.

Professor Sheila Wolfendale has been a primary school, remedial teacher and educational psychologist in several local education authorities. Currently she directs postgraduate educational psychology programmes at the University of East London. Sheila has written many books and articles on areas of special needs, early years, parental involvement, parenting support, family literacy, and baseline assessment and is also the author of the parent-completed profile *All About Me*. She has acted as consultant to LEAs and has contributed to development work on family literacy and parental involvement in a number of other countries. Recent edited books include *Meeting Special Needs in the Early Years, Directions in Policy and Practice* and *Parenting Education and Support, New Opportunities* (1999).

Foreword

OMEP is an international organisation, founded 50 years ago, with the aim of supporting young children within the context of their family and community, wherever and whoever they may be. Along with UNESCO, of which it is an NGO (Non-Governmental Organisation) with consultative status, members have been involved in many aspects of work for and with young children. As an 'enabling' organisation, OMEP functions by initiating communication between countries and individuals. Publication of material is one way in which this is most productive. Over the years many aspects of work involved in the care and education of young children have been addressed by the multidisciplinary membership. Children with special educational needs is one such important issue, not only in the United Kingdom, but worldwide.

In the UK, there has been a long tradition, both within the state and voluntary sectors, of making provision for children identified as having special educational needs. Support for the family and encouragement for the children have been the cornerstones of such provision. Society has moved away from the isolating and institutionalising of such children. There is a recognition that at some time in their lives many children of all abilities will have a 'special' need. Enshrined in the Convention on the Rights of the Child, is the right of all children to education, matched to their ability. For many years in the UK, 'Special Education' has been marked by dedication, determination and above all a realistic and practical approach to the challenges posed by the children and the hope of their families.

When Professor Wolfendale embarked on this project, designed to celebrate achievements in the field, it was to the members of OMEP UK that she turned. Their enthusiastic response has produced a volume which is sure to serve as an inspiration to carers and educators, whatever their field. The examples quoted reveal some of the good practice which exists in the UK today. When visiting schools or being involved at whatever level in special education, one cannot help but be impressed by the joyous approach to life, the enthusiasm with which children approach tasks and the imagination and dedication shown by those involved in the development of the children – parents, teachers and carers – much of which is reflected in the examples contained in this volume.

The thanks of OMEP are due not only to Professor Wolfendale and her army of contributors, but also to the publishers, RoutledgeFalmer. Their co-operation has been invaluable and will almost certainly make the work available to a wider audience, which it truly deserves. In these difficult times, when so much is being expected of practitioners in all fields of care and education, such a partnership is invaluable, bringing to bear, as it does, a different professional element demanding clarity and quality of input.

In producing this volume it is hoped that parents and professionals of all disciplines will be inspired to celebrate the successes of the current good practice described and to build on them. It is often said of children in need of this kind of help, that they are 'special'. Much of what is written here adds depth of meaning to the oft quoted mantras 'each according to his/her ability' 'realising his/her full potential' for indeed special children are deserving of special help. OMEP is grateful to everyone concerned in the production of this volume and hopes that others will be inspired by the content and relate the underlying philosophy to their own work. The contributors would be interested to share experiences with others who are engaged in this absorbing, demanding work.

Margaret Hewitt,
on behalf of the National Executive Committee of OMEP UK

Chapter 1

Profiling early years and special needs

Celebrations of practice

Sheila Wolfendale

Introducing the book

This book celebrates good and innovative practice in the area of early years and special needs. It brings together authors who are practitioners or researchers from a range of different and diverse early-years/pre-school settings, including nurseries, units, and special needs provision. They describe their work with or on behalf of young children who have different and distinctive special needs and disabilities.

The profile of special needs in the early years has risen recently, as a consequence of special educational needs legislation, increased provision to meet special needs in the early years and growing expertise and skills on the part of early-years workers and practitioners. The Government requires early-years providers to be able to meet children's special needs in their settings, and local early-years partnerships must state how providers can meet special needs.

This chapter aims, first of all, to introduce the reader to the thematic organisation of the book, and then goes on to consider a number of key developments in the broad area of early years and special needs which, collectively, attest to a demonstrable shift in policy and practice at all levels of provision.

Themes and topics

The chapters are grouped into four main areas. The first three chapters describe centre-based provision for young children with special educational needs. Pamela Stanier gives an account of a special nursery centre, Moira Evans and colleagues use a case study approach to recount how a young child with Down's Syndrome is integrated into an under-fives education centre, and Pamela Barnes presents issues to do with working with the young child with special needs in the hospital setting.

The second main theme is that of early intervention approaches with a focus on working with parents. Two chapters epitomise this theme: Joy Jarvis and Karen Riley describe how parents of young children developed a support group and Fleur Griffiths gives an account of parental involvement in a multi-professional intervention for pre-school children with communication difficulties.

A third theme explored in the next two chapters takes a questioning and conceptual approach to early-years and special needs phenomena. Helen Penn asks 'what is normal?' and her chapter reviews ideas about normality and disability, taking an international perspective. Theodora Papatheodorou looks at the underlying principles of a number of different theoretical approaches to behaviour problems in the early years and the relevance of such conceptualisations to management approaches.

A fourth major theme is that of research illuminating and developing practice. Three chapters illustrate this symbiotic relationship. Wendy Lynas and Susan Turner describe a research study into early intervention for hearing-impaired children in families of ethnic minority origin. Andrew Lockett takes a critical, research-based look at assessment practice, and Jo Fieldhouse and colleagues describe how the Effective Early Learning Project was adopted and trialled for use by teachers and families working with young children with special educational needs.

The final chapter, written by Sylvia Walker and colleagues, reflects contemporary approaches to collaboration and partnership work between and among 'stakeholders' and providers.

Collectively the chapters exemplify contemporary practice, and an increasing, pervasive profile of special needs within the early-years realm. The provision-based chapters mirror moves towards inclusive educational practice, as other examples attest (Dickins and Denziloe 1998: Alderson 1999) and the research and practice-linked chapters likewise attest to a growing acceptance of evidence-based practice. These and other themes are explored below.

'Snapshots of practice', the subtitle of this book, reflects early-years/special needs practice at this point in time. We hope that the book will serve the dual purpose of encapsulating current work by practitioners and researchers, and providing inspiration for the direction of future provision.

Reconsidering the state and status of special educational needs (sen) in the early years

An earlier text (Wolfendale 1997a) examined how, over recent years, the status of SEN in the early years has risen. This author traces how special educational needs legislation has incorporated key provisions for assessing special needs and for subsequent intervention, and how the Department for Education and Employment's 1994 Code of Practice provided a blueprint for action. Its section, 'Assessments and statements for under fives' incorporated early years/SEN into the overall staged framework of the code.

A revised Code of Practice will come into effect during the academic year 2000–2001 and the revised under-fives section will contain guidance that reflects the implications of recent policy developments in relation to the under fives. For example, since the advent of the Code of Practice in 1994, the requirement to have 'due regard' to its provisions was extended to private nurseries and all under-fives providers. Also, local Early Years Development and Childcare Partnerships must, within their Plans, indicate how children with SEN will be catered for within both childcare and early education. Likewise Baseline Assessment schemes (mandatory for children on entry to school since 1998) accredited by the Qualifications and Curriculum Authority (QCA, see references) must be sensitive to SEN. Such schemes should show teachers which pupils need a targeted teaching strategy or further classroom-based assessment, perhaps leading to specific support from the school or from other agencies.

QCA has also revised the Desirable Outcomes for Children's Learning, creating a foundation stage and reforming early learning goals for the end of the reception year. The revised Desirable Outcomes (QCA 1999) are more sensitive than was the first version to the need to identify special educational needs as early on as possible, and the curriculum guidance and exemplar materials reflect this. This guidance will also be reflected within the revised Code of Practice.

The Government's Green Paper on SEN (DfEE 1997) referred to 'the new emphasis' being placed on early identification and intervention. Its philosophy was expressed thus: 'early diagnosis and appropriate intervention improve the prospects of children with SEN and reduce the need for expensive interventions later on. For some children, giving more effective attention to early signs of difficulties can prevent the development of SEN' (DfEE 1997: 13).

This rhetoric was followed up in the Government's *Programme of Action* (DfEE 1998a) which cross-refers to initiatives, such as Early Years Development and childcare plans referred to above, and also to SURE START (see p. 7).

Many readers will have witnessed and contributed to the rising profile of SEN in the early years and the initiatives reported in this book provide evidence of a widespread view that this area is no longer marginalised and of low priority.

Vulnerability in the early years: towards an inclusive view

During the 1980s and 1990s there was much discussion and debate in professional literature about the precise definition of 'special needs', 'special educational needs', the term used in the 1981 (then 1993, now subsumed into the 1996) Education Act, and 'in need' the definitional term adopted in the 1989 Children Act.

Distinct unease about such labels has pervaded practice too, but practitioners, often working within the legislative frameworks, have had to adopt a pragmatic, accepting attitude. Sue Roffey (1999: 14) provides a useful summary table showing the legislative guidance, including recent early-years legislation and provision. In fact, the 1994 *Code of Practice*, with its comprehensive descriptors of different 'conditions', wittingly or unwittingly brought back the notion of 'categories'.

The DfEE Green Paper, referred to above, draws attention to the legal definition of 'special educational needs' but at the same time points out that this term 'can be misleading and lead to unhelpful assumptions' (DfEE 1997: 12). The fact that SEN is a slippery, elusive concept is borne out by the remark that appears later on the same page:

> whether or not a child has SEN will therefore depend both on the individual and on local circumstances. It may be entirely consistent with the law for a child to be said to have SEN in one school, but not in another.
>
> (DfEE 1997: 12)

As far as young children with identified or suspected SEN are concerned, the Green Paper is of the view that they are at an educational disadvantage, and not surprisingly this theme is echoed in the SEN *Programme of Action* (DfEE 1998a), where the premium is on early identification and intervention.

Implicit in the various conceptions of 'special needs' and 'educational disadvantage', is the vulnerability of young children thus designated. Sinclair *et al.* (1997) depict the journey through childhood using a Snakes and Ladders metaphor, which graphically describes the early or endemic vulnerability of some children, disadvantaged socially, economically, educationally.

Recent government and local initiatives now acknowledge explicitly that provision targeted at young children and their families (Carpenter 1997) cannot effectively be uni-dimensional, that is, the monopoly of one statutory service. The idea of 'joined up' policies epitomises joint service planning and delivery, with the full inclusion of all partners, or 'stakeholders', as all participants are sometimes described. Most chapters in this book epitomise inclusivity and partnership and are vibrant examples of how policies 'trickle down' to practice settings where practitioners and children alike spend their working days.

The coherence of a number of themes denoting partnership approaches towards young children and their families is explored below.

Intervention and prevention: an inclusive approach

Early intervention typically has these primary goals:

- to support families to support their children's development
- to promote children's development in key domains (cognitive, social, physical, emotional, linguistic)
- to promote children's coping competence
- to prevent the emergence of future problems

In the early-years/SEN realm intervention is purposeful and designed to effect as close a match as possible between a young child's identified special needs and that provision or resource which will meet his or her needs and best facilitate learning and development. The interventions should manifestly *make a difference* (see Soriano 1998 for a review of early intervention trends in seventeen European countries).

The recognition that intervening early on in the lives of vulnerable 'at risk' children is socially and educationally justifiable has been the primary rationale behind many social and educational initiatives for around thirty years (see also Wolfendale and Bryans 1979). Often these intiatives were not sustained once initial government start-up grant had been used up and there was insufficient commitment to ensure that the early-years area remained a priority for funding and investment.

It could be argued that similar contemporary initiatives constitute 'old wine in new bottles', but what seems different now is a far broader, encompassing consensus view that concerned efforts will reap dividends.

In a keynote speech at a conference on early intervention (Bayley 1999) the Minister, Paul Boateng, stated that the Government's political agenda in this field includes early intervention, healthy living, community support, multi-agency working and a focus on families. Specifically, the ideals are translated into initiatives such as Education and Health Action Zones, Early Excellence Centres, Childcare Partnerships, SURE START, parenting support, action on school exclusion and many others. Finally, after many years, there is acknowledgement that 'top down' policies are the vital prerequisite for 'on the ground' action.

In this vision, no one service has a monopoly. Indeed, in the blueprint espoused by Mooney and Munton (1997) there are overarching and interrelated principles that should constitute the agenda for a unified approach for early childhood services, comprising:

- how to help parents balance employment and family life
- conceptualisation of early-years services
- facilitating good practice in early childhood services
- considering children's views
- appropriateness of market models of service provision
- the role of government

Utting (1998) echoes some of these themes in his own blueprint for the future of children's services but, in a reference to the short-lived nature of many erstwhile early intervention projects, cautions 'Good practice needs to be secured against political change by seeking cross-party support and an accompanying long-term commitment to funding' (Utting 1998: 13).

To summarise this section, then, there is a contemporary view that children's services should be *co-ordinated* and *targeted* to those children who, within a generalised concept of 'need',

(a) have early-appearing/early identified disabilities and special (educational) needs
(b) are deemed to be vulnerable and at risk by virtue of (a) and/or who
(c) live in milieux of social and economic deprivation and disadvantage.

Features of an inclusive approach to meeting SEN in the early years

I have already indicated how recent and current approaches to early identification and intervention are being perceived as 'inclusive' by virtue of inter-agency collaboration and a 'holist' approach to meeting special needs, particularly in the early years.

As far as inclusion within educational settings is concerned, there is a burgeoning literature (Ainscow *et al.* 1999, Sebba and Sachdev 1997 to name but two; see also Alderson 1999) and a government commitment to promoting inclusion of children with special needs within education. This blueprint, as spelled out in the Green Paper (DfEE 1997) and the SEN *Programme of Action* (DfEE 1998a) envisages a range of approaches to inclusion.

The broadest view of inclusion is expressed thus by Widdows

> it embraces the functioning of families and of societies. In the context of families with disabled children, especially young children, it covers such everyday but important issues as the role of families and friends, and the assistance and support they provide; the impact of disability and non-disabled siblings; the practicality of getting out and about on family outings; the way in which intervention is organised; and the impact of attitudes held by the general public.
>
> (Widdows 1997: 12)

This is the context within which Dickens and Denziloe (1998) couch their myriad of practical proposals as to how to operate inclusion within early-years settings. Their handbook outlines inclusion principles before detailing their proposals within a range of assessment and curriculum areas.

All models and variations of inclusion have in common a view that parental and child involvement is paramount and a key feature of effective inclusion practice. These crucial components are explored below as part of the remit of this chapter, which is to assess the state and status of SEN in the early years.

Parents, families and the SEN

The transition of the erstwhile view that parents are clients and recipients of services towards a view that they should be partners in the planning and delivery of services has been well chronicled (Wolfendale 1983, Wolfendale 1992, Wolfendale 1997b). The philosophy of partnership is expressed within the 1994 SEN *Code of Practice* (DfEE 1994) and the previous government encouraged parent-professional partnership through various means including the Parent Partnership Scheme, which was evaluated for the DfEE by Wolfendale and Cook (1997) and which has been further encouraged by the present government by its inclusion within the SEN *Programme of Action* (DfEE 1998a).

Such realisation that parents are informed experts on their children is belated but totally welcome, as is the recognition that parental representation must form part of local early-years partnerships. Indeed, as a part of 'joined up' approaches, the Government has an 'involving parents' pervasive policy across a number of educational and social welfare areas, of which the main ones in education are:

- family literacy and family numeracy, part of the National Literacy and National Numeracy Strategies
- home-school agreements: from September 1999 all schools are required by law to have one in place
- inclusion of parents' views as part of Baseline Assessment, mentioned at the beginning of this chapter
- partnership in SEN

Cross-departmental (Education, Health, Home Office) parent and family-focussed initiatives include:

- encouragement of parenting education and support programmes (see also Wolfendale and Einzig 1999)
- the creation, during 1999, of the National Family and Parenting Institute, designed ultimately to offer more support to parents for their child-rearing responsibilities
- the initiative of SURE START

SURE START is an innovation which bears some resemblance to previous early-years intervention programmes, wherein parents, as 'first educators', were targetted as recipients of information, support and guidance, to assist them to (a) optimise their very young children's developmental, learning and social potential and (b) to improve upon their parenting and child-rearing skills. As a multi-million pound programme aimed at parents of new-born and pre-school children, SURE START is predicated upon classic prevention principles – prevention of a range of SEN and social problems. It is in part based on longitudinal data that shows some of the early precursors to later educational failure and social exclusion (Rutter 1988, Parsons and Bynner 1998) as well as on a moral, principled commitment towards improving the quality of childhood for many young children. The aim is to improve the life chances of young children, through better access to early education, health services, family support and advice on nurturing.

So, typical SURE START programmes, which initially are based on a number of existing, innovative approaches designed as Trailblazers, will provide: outreach and home visiting, support to families, support for good-quality play, learning and childcare experiences for young children, advice about child and family health, and support for families with young children with special needs.

It can be seen that the premium within SURE START is on family-focussed provision, and this is consistent with other, parallel service provision developments, some of which were mentioned just above. However, it remains to be seen as to whether this governmental flagship enterprise will epitomise a real partnership with parents by consulting with and including them from the earliest planning stages, through service delivery to evaluation, as exhorted by Ball (1997), Dale (1996) and Wolfendale (1999).

However, whether or not truly egalitarian models of parental partnership pertain, for young children with SEN the 'primary professional role is to support the family in making decisions and stating individual preferences regarding services for their children' (Talay-Ongan, 1998: 297).

Taking account of children's views

It was posited earlier that children themselves are important 'stakeholders' in their own learning and education. This principle was fully expounded in the 1994 SEN *Code of Practice* (DfEE 1994) and will be further emphasised within the revised Code of Practice.

Why should we listen to children and take notice of their views? After all, it is adults who have the responsibility for their upbringing, care, welfare and education and we assume that children are too inexperienced in life and too cognitively immature to be able to contribute informed perspectives or to contribute to decision-making on their behalf. Evidence is beginning to suggest otherwise. The rationale and justification for including children's views and consulting them are three-fold: on equal opportunities grounds, on educational grounds and on psychological grounds.

- *On equal opportunities grounds*: children have the right to be listened to and to participate; children are and should be equal partners in the education process; Section 12 of the United Nations Convention in the Rights of the Child is the child's right to be listened to.
- *On educational grounds*: knowing and understanding what children think helps to plan educational experiences better and to make a better match between task and learner; children become more involved and engaged if their views are taken into account; children make better educational progress if they are listened to and their views respected.
- *On psychological grounds*: direct, active involvement in learning increases learning rate and output; cognitive engagement in tasks increases likelihood of effective learning; social engagement with adults (via a dialogue based on children's views) enhances the teacher–pupil relationship and enhances learning.

On the two major spheres of children's experience, namely home and school, we have evidence of young children's ability to express their views, as these examples show:

I Listening to children's views on their home life and families

A recent book has explored the views of children of varying ages on a whole range of domestic topics. Kitzinger and Kitzinger (1990) explored: 'learning to be good, food, lies and secrets, sex and birth, friends, death, religion, politics and prejudice'. The authors say that they learned so much about children's views on family life and how important it is to take these into account when planning child and family-friendly social and employment policies, including child-care, and conclude that 'children do not inhabit a separate world from adults and cannot be sheltered from reality' (ibid: 284). The more we know and understand their likes, dislikes, fears, etc., the better we can prepare children for life and to deal with those realities.

Another approach aimed jointly at parents and young children in eliciting their views about home events and relationships is the parent and child-completed developmental profile developed by this author, entitled *All About Me* (Wolfendale 1998). Extensive work with this profile confirms that very young children aged between three and five years old can describe their feelings about family events and relationships and their self-perception about their own developing skills.

2 Children's views about school and their educational progress

The National Society for the Prevention of Cruelty to Children (NSPCC 1995) undertook a consultation to find out from children what they think about school. Are we surprised to find out that pupils of all ages are insightful and perceptive about what makes a good or a bad teacher; homework and how useful it is; adequate or inadequate resourcing for education; friendship; bullying? One of the main recommendations emerging from this consultation study is that schools should find a method of consulting pupils regularly.

Ann Sherman (1997) observed and interviewed 50 five year-old children during their first term of school. She asked them 'Why do we go to school?' and 'Who makes us go to school?' Their answers are a fascinating illumination of their developing views; here are some replies to the question 'Why do we go to school?'

'we need to go to school to do some learning and working and if we don't do that then we will never get to the bigger school'

'I need to go to school so that my mum can get some peace and quiet'

'to practice for working when you are older'

'well, it's for working and you have your lunch there'

(Sherman 1997: 120)

The Daycare Trust (1999) asked three and four year-olds who attended nurseries about their experiences and elicited full and detailed statements about friends, food, toys, play, and learning. The practical handbook by Miller (1997) shows how young children under the age of eight years can participate, make decisions and take responsibility for their actions.

There is then, much evidence-based practice (see also Utting 1999) in the area of listening to young children, to justify their direct inclusion in decision-making in a number of aspects of their own learning and social experiences.

Assuring quality and effectiveness in early years provision

> Children and their families have a right to expect that our interventions in their lives will be based on the best available knowledge.
>
> (Macdonald and Roberts 1995: 3)

Ways of measuring quality in early-years SEN services were explored in Wolfendale (1997). Models vary in their emphasis and components, but an ever-present reality are the regimes for inspecting nursery settings. At the time of writing, nursery settings can be subject to various types of statutory inspection from OFSTED or from Social Services, the content and range of which vary considerably. During the summer of 1999 the government announced that there will be one unified inspection regime for nurseries and other early-years provision under the overall control and jurisdiction of OFSTED.

Whether or not a revised inspection model will include all components of a quality assurance system remains to be seen. These would include parents' and children's views, staff development, self-appraisal, in addition to the indicators typically incorporated into inspections (Jamieson and Owen 1999).

As the earlier quotation from Macdonald and Roberts indicates, a key way of assessing quality and effectiveness is via evidence-based practice. Such an approach behoves all early-years providers initially to adhere closely to the guidance on *Early Years Development and Childcare Partnership* (DfEE 1998b) especially in respect of SEN (ibid, annexe 8: 30), to set clear goals for curriculum planning and intervention approaches, and to devise outcome measures and means of evaluating these strategies.

There is ever-increasing emphasis upon accountability of professional activities and the broad context here is the set of responsibilities for SEN that local education authorities (LEAs) have and must be seen to exercise equitably (Audit Commission 1999).

Investing in childhood: returns and dividends

Contemporary perspectives on early intervention for all children deemed vulnerable increasingly incorporate a longitudinal and interrelated view of childhood, which has typically been construed as the key first stage of a 'lifespan' perspective. Incorporated into the lifespan model is an entitlement to 'lifelong learning' which should run in parallel with childcare planning. This model is explored by Jamieson and Owen (1999) who say 'Learning becomes an activity, that links people – adults and children alike' (ibid: 79). Thus the growth cycle, of which we are all part, would be explicitly inter-linked, meeting children's developmental and learning needs as well as adults'. In this conception, exisiting parental educational, social and economic disadvantage can be concurrently tackled alongside programmes designed for their children, as exemplified by existing family literacy and numeracy approaches and SURE START.

Building in early intervention/prevention approaches as an integral part of educational provision which are multi-agency and 'holistic' (see DfEE 1998a) represents an inclusive approach to special needs. Taking the long view, Wilson (1998) examines the cost-saving and investment nature of early intervention and goes on to exemplify how differentially targetted programmes can (a) be predicated on theoretical principles and 'best practice' and (b) be financially efficient.

On the issue of dividends (returns from investment) Lloyd et al. (1997) say

> Since we know that risks for poor later outcomes accumulate over time, the benefits of early interventions must not be underestimated. Just as early problems may have long-term effects, early interventions may help children and young people to accrue the social capital needed for good long-term outcomes.
>
> (Lloyd et al. 1997: 10)

Although these authors are proponents of evidence-based interventions, they acknowledge the values and principles behind early intervention rationales: 'The full benefits of investment in children are genuinely immeasurable. Any arguments produced to support investment in our children in essence remain value-based' (ibid: 11).

An encompassing view of childhood and of meeting young children's needs

The *raison d'être* of this book is an affirmation of emerging and effective practice in the area of young children with special needs. The 'snapshots' in the book title are more like moving images than they are static reflections. The chapter authors have created a composite portrait of provision at the end of the twentieth century.

Innovation at any one point in time provides the seeds, not only for what becomes later routine provision, but for future initiatives. Our snapshot-in-time can be compared with erstwhile provision for young children with special needs, characterised as it was largely by separatism, unequal opportunities, parental exclusion. We have come a long way.

Nowadays, theoretical formulations of childhood do not exclude, as a separate category, children with special needs — inclusivity means taking an over-arching view of similar, perhaps universal learning, social, other needs of all children, at whatever fast or slower developmental pace they progress. Differentiation means responding sensitively at critical points in time towards individual children. Wilson (1998) refers to 'teachable moments', a familiar notion to early-years workers, which surely apply to all children. She also draws attention to an historical separation between the traditions of early childhood educators and those of special educators and proposes a realignment and merger of these two disciplines. The key element of her proposed merger is to move beyond 'multi-disciplinary' approaches in which practitioners/professionals work alongside each other (but retain their own approaches) towards a 'transdisciplinary' model. This would require a significant shift for practitioners in the United Kingdom and Ruth Wilson's model is defined and outlined here, to promote and stimulate debate about its efficacy in practice. She writes

> Transdiscipline involves a crossing of disciplinary lines, a stretching of one's professional role, and the development of additional competencies. For the early childhood educator, this means learning more about children with special needs and developing the skills to effectively modify the program for them. For the early childhood special educator this means learning more about human development during the early childhood years, becoming more familar with the intricacies of developmentally appropriate practices, and learning how to work with a larger group of children with varying interests and abilities.
>
> (Wilson 1998: 15)

But perhaps this model is not so radical, proposed as it is at a time when support services are moving closer to each other, in ethos, principles and goals. As stated in McNair (1998: 68) 'many people now expect to work in more than one occupational arena with children and young people during their working lives. The development of the responsive, reflective and skilful practitioner is a challenge faced by everyone'. The interdisciplinary framework conceptualised within this publication is based on the assumption that all those who work with children and young people need similar underpinning knowledge and under-standing. The working metaphor for the framework is the concept of cog wheels – move one and all others move. The 'cogwheel' represents the developmental nature of childhood within its social and cultural context. The metaphor is fully explored and explained within McNair (1998). Suffice to say that it is an image with which to close this introductory chapter. The stories described within this book reflect young children's unique circumstances and needs and how adults and society attempt to provide for these. We bequeath these ideas and strategies to future early-years workers in the new century.

References

Ainscow, M., Farrell, P., Tweddle, D. and Malki, G. (1999) *Effective Practice in Inclusion and in Special and Mainstream Schools Working Together*, Centre for Educational Needs, University of Manchester.

Alderson, P. (ed.) (1999) *Learning and Inclusion: the Cleves School Experience*, London: David Fulton Publishers.

Audit Commission (1999) *Held in Trust, the LEA of the Future*, London.

Ball, M. (1997) *Consulting with Parents, Guidelines for Good Practice*, London: The National Early Years Network.

Bayley, R. (ed.) (1999) *Transforming Children's Lives: the Importance of Early Intervention*, London: Family Policy Studies Centre.

Carpenter, B. (ed.) (1997) *Families in Context: Emerging Trends in Family Support and Early Intervention*: London, David Fulton Publishers.

Dale, N. (1996) *Working with Families of Children with Special Needs*, London: Routledge.

Daycare Trust (1999) *Listening to Children: Young Children's Views on Childcare: a Guide for Parents*, London.

Department for Education and Employment (1994) *Code of Practice on the Identification and Assessment of Special Educational Needs*, London: Stationery Office.

—— (1997) Green Paper, *Excellence for All Children, Meeting Special Educational Needs*, London: Stationery Office.

—— (1998a) *Meeting Special Educational Needs, a Programme of Action*, London: Stationery Office.

—— (1998b) *Early Years Development and Childcare Partnership, Planning Guidance 1999–2000*, London: Stationery Office.

Dickens, M. and Denziloe, J. (1998) *All together – how to create inclusive services for disabled children and their families: a practical handbook for early years workers*, London: National Early Years Network.

Jamieson, A. and Owen, S. (1999) 'Early Enterprise: a New Framework for Early Years and Lifelong Learning', in D. Utting, (ed.) *Children's Services, Now and in the Future*, London: National Children's Bureau.

Kitzinger, S. and Kitzinger, C. (1990) *Talking with Children about Things that Matter*, London: Pandora.

Lloyd, E., Hemingway, M., Newman, T., Roberts, H. and Webster, A. (1997) *Today and Tomorrow, Investing in our Children*, Essex: Barnardos.

Macdonald, G. and Roberts, H. (1995) *What Works in the Early Years: Effective Interventions for Children and their Families in Health, Social Welfare, Education and Child Protection*, Essex: Barnardos.

McNair, S. (ed.) (1998) *Developing Disciplines, the Experience of the Discipline Networks Programme 1995–98*, Suffolk: DfEE Publications.

Miller, J. (1997) *Never Too Young, How Young Children Can Take Responsibility and Make Decisions*, London: National Early Years Network.

Mooney, A. and Munton, A. (1997) *Research and Policy in Early Childhood Services; Time for a New Agenda*, University of London Institute of Education.

NSPCC (1995) *A Child's View of School – Consulting Pupils to Create a Listening and Responsive School*, London.

Parsons, S. and Bynner, J. (1998) *Influences on Adult Basic Skills*, London: Basic Skills Agency.

Qualifications and Curriculum Authority (QCA) *The National Framework for Baseline Assessment; Criteria and Procedures for the Accreditation of Baseline Assessment Schemes*, London.

QCA (1999) *Early Learning Goals*, London: QCA.

Roffey, S. (1999) *Special Needs in the Early Years, Collaboration, Communication and Co-ordination*, London: David Fulton Publishers.

Rutter, M. (1988) *Studies of Psycho-Social Risk: the Power of Longitudinal Data*, Cambridge: Cambridge University Press.

Sebba, J., and Sachdev, D. (1997) *What Works in Inclusive Education?* Essex: Barnardos.

Sherman, A. (1997) 'Five year olds' perception of why we go to school', *Children and Society*, 11 (2): 117–28.

Sinclair, R., Hearn, B. and Pugh, G. (1997) *Preventive Work with Families, the Role of Mainstream Services*, London: National Children's Bureau.

Soriano, V. (ed.) (1998) *Early Intervention in Europe, Trends in 17 European Countries*, Middlefart, Denmark: European Agency for Development in Special Needs Education.

Talay-Ongan, A. (1998) *Typical and Atypical Development in Early Childhood*, Leicester: British Psychological Society Books.

Utting, D. (ed.) (1998) *Children's Services, Now and in the Future*, London: National Children's Bureau.

Widdows, J. (1997) *A Special Need for Inclusion*, London: Children's Society.

Wilson, R. (1998) *Special Educational Needs in the Early Years*, London: Routledge.

Wolfendale, S. (1983) *Parental participation in Children's Development and Education*, London: Gordon and Breach Publications.

—— (1992) *Empowering Parents and Teaching – Working for Children*, London: Cassell.

—— (1998) *All About Me*, Nottingham: NES-Arnold.

—— (1999) 'Parents as key determinants in planning and delivering parenting education and support programmes: an inclusive ideology', in S. Wolfendale and H. Einzig (eds) *Parenting Education and Support – New Opportunities*, London: David Fulton Publishers.

—— (ed.) (1997a) *Meeting Special Needs in the Early Years, Directions in Policy and Practice*, London: David Fulton Publishers.

—— (ed.) (1997b) *Working with Parents of SEN Children after the Code of Practice*, London: David Fulton Publishers.

Wolfendale, S. and Bryans, T. (1979) *Early Identification of Learning Difficulties, a Model for Intervention*, Tamworth: National Association for Special Educational Needs.

Wolfendale, S. and Cook, G. (1997) *Evaluation of SEN Parent Partnership Schemes*, DfEE Research Report No. 34, Suffolk: DfEE Publications.

Wolfendale, S. and Einzig, H. (eds) (1999) *Parenting Education and Support, New Opportunities*, London: David Fulton Publishers.

Chapter 2

Working together in different ways
Rodney House School

Pamela Stanier

This chapter is a description of Rodney House School, which is a special nursery provision in Manchester. In it I explain how we work with very young children with special needs, and how we assess children in an inter-disciplinary context. I examine the ways in which the day-to-day life of the school is informed by the staff's philosophy of education and our view of special educational needs.

The school has forty full-time equivalent places, although there are sixty children on roll, as many of the children attend for only part of each week. They come from all parts of the city, and have a wide range of special educational needs. Some are profoundly disabled, and for these children we plan a sensory and early communication curriculum; some have broad developmental delay, which may be moderate or severe; there are some children with physical disabilities and some with language disorders or emotional and behavioural difficulties. These children follow a differentiated early-years curriculum. In addition, we have a small class for children who have major communication difficulties within the autistic spectrum; this class follows a programme which offers a highly structured approach with an augmented communication system; the teaching methods in this class draw largely on the TEACCH programme.[1]

The youngest children attend on a part-week basis and spend the rest of the week at home. Most of the older children have full-time places, or also attend another establishment nearer to home on their other days, to provide social integration and to maintain links with their local community. The school has four classes, arranged chronologically, with a 'young nursery' class for the youngest and most vulnerable children with profound difficulties; a nursery class, which is integrated with a playgroup for six local children each day; a reception/ Year 1 class, and the TEACCH group.

In this chapter I offer my interpretation of the ways in which the school and its allied medical provision is seen from a number of different perspectives, starting

---

[1] TEACCH: Treatment and Education of Autistic and Related Communication-Handicapped Children, a structured and visually based system for working with individuals within the autistic spectrum; developed by Eric Schopler in Carolina USA in the sixties.

as it were from a distance, and working in to the heart of the school. I envisage the perceptions of outsiders, the LEA, visitors, parents and children, the staff, medical colleagues, and myself.

From the perspective of the Local Education Authority

Rodney House was built in the 1960s and was then part of the Health Department's provision for 'handicapped children', for it was originally established by parents of children with cerebral palsy, using funds raised by the Spastics Society, now called Scope. It was recognised as a 'hospital school' in the late 1970s, by the Department for Education and Science, now the Department for Education and Employment. Although the hospital which it served closed over a decade ago, the building still belongs to the Health Authority and the school is a tenant within the building.

The school is a maintained special school in inner-city Manchester and is one of four assessment provisions in the city. These were established by the city council in response to the 1981 Education Act to provide an assessment resource for children under five years old. Each of the assessment provisions has aspects in common with the others but all differ in significant ways: one is part of a nursery school, two are part of mainstream primary schools, and Rodney House stands alone with important features which distinguish it from the other schools. At Rodney House there is a nurse permanently on site, as well as speech and language therapists and physiotherapists who are based in the building, rather than working on a peripatetic basis as in other special schools.

The LEA has an Admissions Panel for assessment provision, which meets each half term. At these meetings, the Headteachers and other members of the group – a paediatrician, an educational psychologist, the head of the city's pre-school special needs service, and a clerk from the LEA – consider the information that has come to the LEA under section 332 of the 1996 Education Act, with the referrals from the educational psychologists who have met the children.

Children are then allocated to an appropriate assessment school, usually on a geographical basis, as the schools are based in four quadrants of the city, but with the needs of individual children in mind. Children with more profound difficulties or more challenging children will be allocated to Rodney House because of the higher level of medical input and the more favourable staff:child ratio in the school. Parents are then invited to visit the school and are offered a place for their child; we arrange the transport and children begin their school life.

The education department is also involved through the statutory input of educational psychologists. Each child is admitted at stage 3 or 4 of the code of practice for children with special educational needs and the assessment by the school's educational psychologist is part of the inter-disciplinary assessment, for they provide a summative analysis of each child's capabilities using formal and standardised tests which complement the school's observational approach to assessing children's needs. The psychologist also makes the recommendation to the LEA about the child's needs, in the light of parents' views, the LEA's provision and the school's advice. The LEA role continues in managing the paperwork of the assessment process. Minutes of the review meetings are sent to the office and in the statutory assessment, the administrative staff in the offices take responsibility for collating the paperwork. The LEA is responsible for the final decisions about a child's future school placement once the assessment is completed.

From the perspective of visitors to the school

Visitors who come to the school knowing of its 'health' origins, such as medical students, or health visitors, are often surprised to discover that the school has the appearance and atmosphere of a 'normal' nursery school. The school is not like a clinic or hospital facility: there are bright paintings by children on the walls, interesting displays and a wide range of play resources. The emphasis in the school is education for the children and assessment within an early-years education provision. The children, although clearly having special needs, spend their time in focused play within a friendly and relaxed atmosphere.

From a parent's perspective

When parents are offered a place and visit the school they are often very apprehensive about what they will find; they fear it will be like a clinic or institution of some kind. They too can be reassured by the atmosphere and appearance of the building, which is like any other good early-years establishment, with a wide range of play equipment and activities planned for the children. A parent whose daughter left us to go to another school commented that the new school felt very serious, because all we did at Rodney House was have fun with the children. (As Headteacher I felt that was a two-edged compliment! The 'fun' which exists is the result of a lot of hard work – of which more later.)

Working with parents is an important part of the life of the school. We acknowledge that parents of children with any kind of serious disability can suffer negative emotions such as grief for the 'lost' normal child they expected to have, anger, and despair at the thoughts of the future. Of course they can also display courage, tenacity and pleasure in their own child; not everything is negative. These emotions are complex and part of the role of the school staff is to listen to parents' fears and hopes for the future.

We involve parents in the school in a number of ways. Before coming into the school, the teacher and Headteacher visit the child at home, partly to complete some of the admission paperwork, but also to be able to talk to the family and meet the child on 'their' territory rather than ours. We find that this makes transition into the school easier, and it helps us to see children in their own home where they feel most confident.

Parents come with their child for as long as they like when the child starts school; some children settle very quickly, while others are more anxious. We like parents to stay with their child until they relax and feel confident about the provision. It can be daunting for parents to leave their very disabled child who has taken such a large part in their lives. Although parents do appreciate having time for themselves when they do not have to worry about their child, it is still a wrench to leave them at first and one of our cornerstones is an 'open-door' policy where parents can visit whenever they want and stay as long as they like. This, paradoxically makes parents more confident about *not* coming into school all the time; they know there is nothing hidden from them, and they feel part of the team.

Once a child is attending school regularly, we keep in touch with parents through 'home-school' books, phone calls, home visits and social occasions in the school, and formal reviews, as well as parents visiting when they choose.

At six monthly intervals, we hold a 'family conference' on each child. These meetings include the family, the classteacher, all the therapists involved, the school nurse, health visitor, social worker if applicable, and anyone else whom the parents wish to invite, and we discuss children's progress and plan for their immediate future. These meetings can be daunting for the families, but we hope that, as they already know the 'professionals' involved, the experience will be a useful one. In addition, at the end of each term the teachers prepare an end-of-term report on each child for their family, reporting on how each child has progressed in each of the focus areas and looking at how far they have met their targets. The end-of-term reports have a formative function in informing the development of the individual plans for the next term, and a summative function in summarising what targets each child has achieved.

From the perspective of the staff

Each class has a team of staff, led by a teacher, with a varying staff:child ratio according to the needs of the children. It is the teachers' responsibility to plan all the work for the class and lead the team, deploying staff and observing the children's progress. The other staff share in the planning and make written or verbal observations of the children according to their skills and abilities; although some of the staff have Nursery Nurse Examining Board (NNEB) qualifications, many are untrained when they start at the school and we have a programme of induction and training which provides them with the skills they need and imbues them with the school's ethos. Some staff are working towards NVQ status, as part of the school's policy of developing all its staff.

The staff know that the school's reputation and successes in working with young children rest on them, and are a result of their work. We encourage an open and reflective approach so that the tensions of working with children with challenging behaviours and serious learning difficulties can be acknowledged. It is only through supporting the staff and the staff supporting each other that the school can continue to progress. We have a shared development plan, regular meetings to further the development of the school, a commitment to in-house and off-site training, a reflective management style and opportunities to talk together as class teams and in peer groups of staff doing the same job. These are all important management tools to ensure that the staff are working together.

One of my management tenets is a belief that all people involved in a community such as this want to give of their best to the children and to work well; the staff in the school are important because without their commitment there could be no success in the school.

Each staff member has a different role in the team. The teachers have the most responsibility in leading their class team and planning the work in the class-rooms. Once a child is in school and settled, the teachers draw up an individual education plan for each child to cover a term. These targets in what we call 'Focus Areas' are based on the relevant National Curriculum standards for children of their age, except for the very youngest children with profound and multiple learning difficulties for whom we offer a sensory and early communi-cation curriculum and whose focus sheets are based around development of the senses and of body awareness.

These individual plans are used by the teachers to plan the activities they offer within the framework in the whole-school themes for each term. We find that this makes for a more holistic curriculum and allows staff more fun in planning what they do in the classrooms. We plan the topic for each term as a whole school, using the broad Areas of Learning for the early years as a basis; past terms have covered the themes 'Stories', 'Colour and Patterns', 'Animals' etc. The themes provide a basis for art work and out-of-school visits, stories and imaginative play.

Our assessment of each child takes place, therefore, within the framework of an early-years classroom, and is based on naturalistic observations of children in play situations. We do not take the children out of the room to 'assess' them. These are the strengths of the approach; it relies of course on all the staff having a clear insight into the teaching and learning aims of each of the activities, and on the staff having good knowledge both of child development in the early years and of each child's particular strengths and needs.

From colleagues' perspective

Rodney House has a long 'medical' background and is still a Health Trust owned building. It is a work base for therapy colleagues, such as speech therapists, physiotherapists and paediatricians, all of whom have their own professional standards and ways of working. They also have their own model of disability which is different in significant ways from the education model and I think it important that we acknowledge those differences, to be able to build on the strengths of each role.

The medical model can be seen to be based on a deficiency model. A syndrome, for example, is a collection of defects in a child; things which mar the normality which should exist. The role of the medical personnel is to put things right as far as possible; if there can be no cure, to offer palliative treatment. This is essentially different from the role of education staff, whose aim is to develop each child further. Medical colleagues have different roles in putting together the jigsaw of pieces which complete a full picture of each child. The paediatricians are heavily involved with the children when they are very young and are instrumental in bringing each child to the attention of the Local Education Authority. They monitor child development, and refer children to hospital colleagues if specific investigations or treatment are required. They liaise with general practitioners and can co-ordinate the many varied investigations. There may be regular consultations and intensive investigations while a child is young until a diagnosis is reached but after that the parents and children receive less frequent input from paediatricians. What they do offer is knowledge about a child's medical condition, and significant information about the implications of those medical needs for the child's future education.

The school nurse is an important medical colleague who provides day-to-day input and often makes it possible for children to remain in school. Many of the children receive prescribed drugs for example for epilepsy, or need tube-feeding and her presence in school keeps them safe and healthy. The speech and language therapy colleagues also offer useful guidance about feeding difficulties which children with profound learning difficulties can experience. Children who find it hard to co-ordinate their movements can easily choke during meal times and staff need advice and training in feeding skills which the speech therapists provide, as well as advice about positioning and special equipment from physiotherapists and occupational therapists.

The physiotherapists' input involves treating a child's physical problems and providing advice about positioning children and the use of standing frames, or appropriate seating, often in liaison with occupational therapists. However, physiotherapists do not work with children who are progressing normally and only work with children who have physical difficulties when they feel that their input will make a difference. In working with other children who will never be able to walk, because of their profound developmental delay, the physiotherapists try to prevent the child deteriorating further and improve their quality of life, but do not aim for improvement. Once a child is adequately mobile, their input is no longer necessary. In the educational model, teachers try to improve and develop all children's physical skills and a child's individual education plan, drawn up by the teaching staff, will address the child's developing physical skills.

Similarly, our speech therapy colleagues, while providing useful information about a child's language development, and offering advice for the language areas of a child's individual education plan, do not continue to work with children who are making no progress in their language acquisition. The criterion for continued input from the therapist is that a child's language development is significantly behind their global development. The school's language and communication curriculum offers input for all children. It provides for those whose communication strategies are very limited, and develops the language range of more competent speakers.

Other LEA colleagues who provide continuing advice to the classroom staff are the teachers from a number of services for children with sensory impairments: for hearing-impaired children, for visually-impaired children and for those who have multi-sensory impairments where both hearing and vision difficulties affect their abilities to learn. Staff from these services come into the school to work with individual children and to advise the classroom staff. They provide individual programmes for children, which classroom staff can implement as part of the child's individual education programme, and they provide advice for the statement. Often these peripatetic staff have met the children before they are admitted to the school and have supported parents in the child's earlier days, and this contact continues through the review meetings.

The comparison made above between education and medical perspectives does not mean that the therapy colleagues' contribution is any less important than the teachers'. However, it can be limited, specific and with a short time scale. There are different professional perspectives, but it is important to acknowledge the different contributions made by all professionals within Rodney House as a whole. By working together in different ways, sharing opinions and expertise, both formally and informally, we can do the best for each child.

The co-existence of therapy and medical provision alongside the education of the children is the strength of an inter-disciplinary facility such as Rodney House. We find it of great benefit to the children that therapists based in the building and the school staff can meet and talk together on a day-to-day basis. The therapists can join in classroom meetings, can share their planning and can take part in school events and out-reach facilities, such as the recently started 'afternoon playgroup' for children on the school waiting list or whose parents are anxious about taking them to local mainstream playgroups.

When the physiotherapists and speech therapists are in and out of the classrooms on a regular basis, they become part of the child's daily life in the school. The advantage for the school staff is that advice can be on hand about children's physical needs in the classroom, about children's language development and about how their medical condition can influence their learning. For parents there is no pressure to take their children to any appointments in a clinic, where there may be a difficult journey, a waiting time and a child who is reluctant to work with a relative stranger.

The disciplines meet in our family conferences which provide a formal opportunity for professionals to talk together and with parents about work they have been doing with each child. They provide opportunities for a sharing of joint knowledge, and planning together for a child's needs, so that progress in one area can be used in another, or they can provide information to parents. Speech and language therapists may be able to advise family and school staff together about children's developing language skills and about the use of alternative communication systems, such as signing. Physiotherapists can provide information about how a child can physically access classroom activities. The 'inter-disciplinary' nature of the assessment focuses on these very important family meetings, but is only in addition to the many informal discussions and practical work in the classrooms.

Annette's perspective

To illustrate the work of Rodney House, I shall describe one little girl, Annette. Annette is four years old and is profoundly physically disabled following a precipitate birth and later open heart surgery, possibly during which she suffered an aortic thrombus. The end result of this is that she has quadriplegic hypertonic cerebral palsy. In addition she has an unusual visual condition, with an alternate convergent squint which leads to cross-fixation, and tripartate field vision. She is also unable to speak, because of poor oral control.

The implications for this child have been far-reaching. She is stiff, and has needed regular physiotherapy and a number of surgical interventions to loosen tendons. She has glasses, but is unable to use her eyes for eye-pointing communication because she can neither turn her head nor use her eyes meaningfully. In addition the family has many of the social problems which beset children living in inner-city areas, including poverty, and separated parents. There is however an extended and supportive family which is loving, close, and caring but does not really understand the implications of the child's condition.

Annette was admitted to the school on a part-time place when she was 2 years old, initially on a part-week place, but full-time from when she was 3½ years old. She has been very difficult to assess in terms of her educational needs. She took a long time to settle into the school; at home she had had constant adult attention which led her to see people as her main source of interest and stimulus, and she preferred to watch people than to try to use toys or take part in classroom activities. She found the demands of a school day hard to understand, wanting to be cuddled passively. This is of course understandable given that she is unable to pick up toys easily and use them, and given that she has such difficulty in accessing the world.

It has taken us a long time to learn from Annette herself about what she can do and wants to do, and for us to realise that inside this very damaged body is a child who is able to learn. Part of that realisation has come over a period of time, for on first acquaintance it would seem that she has profound intellectual impairment as well as the physical difficulties.

The team working together has included physiotherapists, speech and language therapists, school nurse, class team and peripatetic teachers of visually impaired children. Annette has had appropriate seating arranged through Disability Services, and has had physiotherapy on a daily basis. The school arranged an outside assessment by the ACE/Access Centre, which assesses children's communication needs and advises on appropriate communication aids.

Following this the class teacher and classroom staff, and the speech therapist, started to work with Annette using Big Mac switches (small switch items which include a tape to record short messages and a large colourful switch which works on one press). This was not entirely suitable because, as the physiotherapists pointed out, Annette becomes more stiff on effort and she was unable to achieve the necessary hand movements reliably. Attaching the switches to Annette's usual Jenx chair was unsuccessful because she would operate the switch involuntarily and therefore become discouraged from using the switch message appropriately.

We therefore purchased a small switch mounted on an angled arm attached to Annette's chair, which required her to make a larger movement. This proved more manageable, but we had to bear in mind that we were working with a very young child and that in a home environment the family are not always able to continue to use the equipment as efficiently as it can be used in the school environment. We also had to ensure that Annette continued to enjoy school life, and was given opportunities for play.

During Annette's time at the school we held review meetings every six months where her progress was discussed, and provided the advice to the LEA about the school provision to meet her needs. The quandary in the assessment was that although Annette had major difficulties in her learning she was, we believed, within a normal intellectual range and therefore her physical difficulties were paramount. This was difficult to assess, because she cannot use toys or school equipment appropriately, and because of her person-oriented interests, she does not readily engage with school activities such as books which do not hold her interest or Information and Communication Technology (ICT) programs.

The phrase 'Severe learning difficulties' is used as a euphemism for 'severely mentally handicapped'. Annette has serious difficulties in accessing learning but does not have learning difficulties in that sense. She needs major support, i.e. small classes and a high level of adult input. In the future she will need access to sophisticated ICT systems which are not readily available in schools or to working-class families, in order to be able to communicate at all. She will need psychological support, because her life will be difficult, and she will need maximum support for her physical needs, in movement, feeding and personal needs.

All these needs have become clearer as a result of the interdisciplinary work within the school.

From a management perspective

This brief and straightforward description of how Rodney House works and what it does, is based on a school philosophy which values each child as an individual personality who will have strengths as well as difficulties, and which sees each child as an individual with a family background, likes and dislikes, preferences and traits rather than foremost a child with a disability. Each child is different.

Two children with an identical syndrome are still quite different personalities, and they are so clearly their parents' children. We try not to forget this.

It seems appropriate to elucidate my own philosophy for working with young children with major learning difficulties. My philosophy has been heavily influenced by the work of educationalists such as Margaret McMillan, Susan Isaacs and Barbara Tizard. As a Headteacher, my aim has been to create a school where there are high standards of early-years education, although the children have such different and serious educational needs.

As a manager I have been particularly influenced by the work of current educational writers including amongst others, Fullan (1991) and Stoll and Fink (1996). I have needed to have a clear vision for the school, to know what high standards are and be able to achieve them. My strategies have included staff development, regular review and monitoring of the curriculum, close liaison with colleagues, outside agencies and other schools, and my own personal professional development, which defines myself as a learner within the school as well as its main leader. In this I have been heavily influenced by the work of Revans, whose 'Action Learning' model is one which I use in staff development and in my own work.

As a practising Buddhist, I have a strong belief in the value of all human experience, even that which stems from disability. As an educationalist, I believe that education is a right for all individuals. It is the responsibility of the school to provide the children and their families with as high a quality of education as we can, so that the children do have 'fun at school', as the parent I mention earlier summarised our work. Our children with special needs are children first.

I have described the medical model as a deficiency model, and the education approach as a developmental model. Learning can be seen as a lifelong experience and challenge which starts at birth. This applies equally to people of all intellectual and physical capacity. Adults working in the school can develop new skills, both practical and intellectual, as well as providing a learning environment for the children in the school.

The school has a duty to continue with children who are making very little and very slow progress, because that is their right as members of society. Starting as we do from where each child is, progress is always possible. For example, a severely disabled child who cannot yet pick up a toy will be encouraged to reach out and grasp attractive items. Further teaching can develop the child's discrimination between items, so that toys are used appropriately, until the child can begin to acquire useful knowledge and skills. If this is not possible because of the child's profound disabilities, then we can continue to work on improving what communication skills the child has by learning to interpret their communications, and help the child begin to express choices in their own, admittedly limited, world.

For older children with moderate difficulties, a slower mainstream curriculum is possible, provided that learning is broken down into small steps. We offer a wide range of early-years experiences, covering all aspects of the curriculum, but acknowledging that children learn at a slow pace. The local children in our integrated playgroup are helped to explore the world around them, and develop a wide range of different skills. All of the children in the school will, we hope, have a relish for life and a desire to learn and achieve no matter what their special needs may be. They are first and foremost young children, with their own personality and strengths; the special needs are only part of the child.

Further reading

Abbott, L. and Rodger, R. (eds) (1994) *Quality Education in the early Years*, Milton Keynes: Open University Press.

Bennett, N., Wood, L. and Rogers, S. (1997) *Teaching Through Play*, Milton Keynes: Open University Press.

Blenkin, G. and Kelly, A. (1992) *Assessment in Early Childhood Education*, London: Paul Chapman Publishing.

Bruce, T. (1992) *Time to Play in Early Childhood Education*, London: Hodder and Stoughton.

David, T. (1995) *Under Five, Under Educated?* Milton Keynes: Open University Press.

Dowling, M. (1988) *Education 3–5; a Teacher's Handbook*, London: Paul Chapman Publishing.

Fullan, M. (1991) *The New Meaning of Educational Change*, London: Cassell.

Hargreaves, D. and Hopkins, D. (1991) *The Empowered School*, London: Cassell.

Isaacs, S. (1960) *Intellectual growth in Young Children*, London: Routledge and Kegan Paul.

McMillan, M. (1930) *The Nursery School*, London: Dent.

Moyles, J. (1992) *Just Playing?* Milton Keynes: Open University Press.

Revans, R. (1983) *The ABC of Action Learning*, London: Chartwell-Bratt.

Stoll, L. and Fink, D. (1996) *Changing Our Schools*, Milton Keynes: Open University Press.

Tizard, B. and Hughes, M. (1984) *Young Children Learning*, London: Fontana.

Whitaker, P. (1993) *Managing Change in Schools*, Milton Keynes: Open University Press.

Chapter 3

Integrating a child with Down's Syndrome into an Under Fives Education Centre

Moira Evans, Moira Keating and Elizabeth Knight

In the United Kingdom (UK) children with Down's Syndrome received no education at all before 1971. Fortunately this is no longer so and Down's Syndrome children generally either receive education in special schools or are integrated within mainstream education. The authors of this chapter believe in integration and agree with studies which have highlighted '. . . the low levels of achievement typical of special school leavers, not because the schools were not trying to help the children reach their potential but because of problems inherent in isolating children from their own neighbourhood and from their peers' (Bird and Buckley 1993: 4).

This chapter has been written by three members of an Under Fives' Education Centre who had the opportunity of integrating a Down's Syndrome Child into their centre. In this chapter we outline what systems we as an institution needed to have in place, the roles of the Special Educational Needs Co-ordinator (SENCO) and other staff and what effect the integration of a Down's Syndrome child would have on the curriculum planning at the centre. We have put this in the context of the system at the time.

The setting

Willow Under Fives' Education Centre is an inner London Council integrated care and education provision for 52 children from 0 to 5 years. The centre was originally a Council Social Services Day nursery which was taken over, along with all the day nurseries in the borough, by the Council's Education Department in the early 1990s. The provision was completely reorganised, the job descriptions and staffing structure were changed and many staff were redeployed or made redundant. The essential criterion of a UK recognised teaching qualification for the post of Head of each Centre and a qualified teacher post were introduced to the structure. These changes were innovative and were welcomed by some, but, nevertheless, brought with them many anxieties and uncertainties. The Management teams in the centres were faced with many challenges whilst trying to manage these changes. It was in this climate that this case study is set.

The borough also drew up a new admission policy, which stated that 30 per cent of the places at Willow were to be reserved for children with special needs.

We were very fortunate that most staff had an interest in working with such children and were in sympathy with the spirit of the recent Green Paper *Excellence in Schools* (DfEE, 1997) which states 'There are strong educational, social and moral grounds for educating pupils with special educational needs in mainstream schools'.

Applying the *Code of Practice*

When the *Code of Practice* was introduced in September 1994 the centre was not obliged to adopt it but we felt that there was no reason why we should not and many reasons, not least good practice, why we should adopt the *Code of Practice*. We recognised that if we were to develop a special educational needs policy for the centre we would need to demonstrate our commitment to it by allocating time and resources. Thus we set about appointing a Special Educational Needs Co-ordinator (SENCO). The Head, the SENCO and the Curriculum Co-ordinator (the teacher at the centre) had much experience of working with children with Special Educational Needs (SEN). They recognised that working with children with SEN requires responses and resources to be co-ordinated, an appropriate curriculum introduced and support systems set up and implemented. They also knew that all concerned needed to be made aware of the systems and why they were in place.

The SENCO and the Head of Centre were sent on courses to familiarise themselves with the *Code of Practice*. Although the Head and SENCO took responsibility for introducing the *Code of Practice* and devising the Special Needs policy, we felt it was very important that they did not develop the policy alone and then impose it on the staff and parents. It was crucial that the whole staff and the parents were involved in the policy and understood the need for it. We allocated an Inservice (INSET) day to work with the staff on the policy, time to work with parents on the policy and time to write and produce the centre's special needs policy. In retrospect we can see that this setting up time was essential if we were to meet the needs of all children at the centre. We were very lucky that the whole staff team was committed to including children with special needs and had experience of working with children with diverse needs. Staff, collectively and individually, had always examined their practice and tried to find ways of meeting the needs of all children.

Despite the commitment to inclusion we still had some problems in devising and introducing our policy. In our meetings with staff about the *Code of Practice* some said they were very concerned about the use of the word 'assessment' at Stage 4, saying that parents would think we were psychologically testing their child and would feel that their child was being labelled. The Head and SENCO argued that the centre had consulted with parents about the policy and felt sure that the majority understood the process and recognised the benefits for their child and explained that very few children would move on to stage 4 or would see a psychologist. Some staff felt that the involvement of the SENCO could undervalue their contribution and that somehow they were not considered skilled enough to plan for the child. The Head and SENCO were able to convince them that this was not the case: what they were aiming for was a coherent approach that co-ordinated the observations and views of all who worked with individual children to produce a plan for each child based on their specific needs. The meetings with the parents about the development of our Special Needs policy and the *Code of Practice* were very well received and the parents said they felt very pleased to be consulted. They felt it was very important to address staff's and parents' concerns at an early stage as they believed that unless everyone involved was fully committed our policy would end up as a printed document in the Head's and SENCO's file and would not be put into practice.

Christina: a case study

As we were going through the process of developing our special needs policy we were asked to offer a place to Christina a 17 month-old Down's Syndrome child. The social worker from the borough's special needs team arrived at the centre with Christina and her grandmother. They had been to other provision in the area but chose Willow because they said it was small and welcoming and they felt was right for Christina and her family. Christina was the child of a teenage mother who was attending a local school. It was very clear from the beginning that Christina had a loving and committed mother and extended family that clearly wanted to work in partnership with the staff to meet Christina's needs.

We were pleased to hear that Christina was to begin at Willow and wanted to be prepared to offer some extra support as appropriate. Christina was admitted to the 0–2 year-olds room when she was just 18 months old. As a centre we could not have wished for a better opportunity to test the effectiveness of our new special needs policy. From the day she was admitted the staff were enthusiastic about providing an appropriate programme for her and, perhaps more import-antly, were very keen to learn from her family and work in partnership with them. Christina was in good health and had recovered well from an operation to correct a faulty heart valve. She had started to walk and wore special boots to help her mobility. She was social and responsive and had some play skills. She understood simple instructions and remembered short sequences in naming and pointing. She had a few words and was finger feeding.

The SENCO initially got in touch with the Down's Syndrome Association for some general advice and explained that she could apply for some additional support hours. They remarked that it was generally important to clearly direct the child's attention to objects and activities and encourage increased duration of attention. They also advised that modelling behaviours and lots of repetition would be the best way to consolidate learning and that enriched early input was the most effective support for children with Down's Syndrome. This information was shared with staff who were preparing for Christina's arrival. It also helped support our first request for additional support time from the borough's under-fives special educational needs panel.

Her grandparents and mother were sharing her care. As well as having a very strong commitment to working with the centre staff they were also working with 'Palace', a local group organised by parents that gives support to Down's Syndrome children and their families. It was agreed that initially Christina would attend Willow on only three days a week. Christina and her grandmother attended 'Palace' on the other two days and were offered massage, physiotherapy, aromatherapy, conductive education and a crèche. This gave the centre a very good link with a valuable local resource. We spoke with Christina's family who were very enthusiastic that we visit when Christina was there. We arranged for the keyworker and the SENCO to visit on separate occasions. They were able to see Christina have a session with a physiotherapist who trained at the Peto Institute in Hungary where a system of movement therapy called 'conductive education' has been developed and liaise with the therapist to gain ideas that could be used at the centre. The challenge for us was how we could ensure that our special needs policy worked to support Christina and how we could best access the family's expertise. The family had been attending 'Palace' for some time and had developed many skills. Margaret, the grandmother who normally picked up and collected Christina was particularly skilled in working with Christina and was a great source of inspiration and support for us.

Initially Christina needed a lot of support to separate from her grandmother who had been a constant presence in her life. She was generally shy to communicate in the centre and would cry when her grandmother left. We worked to enable her to use different forms of communication to make her needs known. We supported her need to extend her physical skills such as her recently acquired ability to walk. Working in a 0–2 year-olds room is especially demanding, as every child needs to have individual attention from staff. We recognised, however, that Christina needed extra help to support her at this crucial stage in her development. So what could we do with the resources we had? We enlisted the help of Margaret who, through her relationship with 'Palace', was able to give staff advice on developing Christina's physical and language skills.

The centre has always believed in a multidisciplinary approach to meeting children's needs but has also recognised that, in practice, usually because of bureaucratic restrictions, it is not always possible. Christina's grandmother helped us bridge the gap between the services. She helped facilitate the arrangements for staff to go to 'Palace' as part of our staff development plan to learn to help Christina physically and in her language development. There was some initial information from Christina's application for a priority place sent to Willow which included a report from the consultant community paediatrician and the social worker that had been working with the family. This supported our liaison with Christina's family and we were put in touch with the specialist speech therapist and the physiotherapist, who were working with the family.

To demonstrate our commitment to including Christina and any future children with Down's Syndrome we felt we had to prioritise training for staff in our staff development plan and allocate extra resources. This also demonstrated to staff our support for them, as all too often staff feel that managers accept children with special needs but staff are then left 'holding the baby'. Children with Down's Syndrome often have language development as the most delayed area and this was true for Christina. Makaton, a form of sign language support, takes advantage of the fact that a child's visual and physical skills precede their speaking and listening abilities. This form of communication helped to support her acquisition of vocabulary and minimise her frustration at not making herself understood. A study by Miller et al. (1991) noted that children with Down's Syndrome can attain a similar level of development to a typically developing child if their signed vocabulary was included. The staff in the 0–2s room had been learning basic signing from Margaret and found it helpful. The staff in the 2–3s room, on hearing this, asked if they could go as a team on a Makaton training course. Fortunately because of our staff development plan we were able to agree to this request. Again this had the added bonus of staff feeling supported as well as feeling more confident in working with Christina. We really began to feel that the whole centre was working very positively as a team to develop Christina's potential to the full and as another added bonus, all the children in the group also had great fun using signs as well as speech. There were children in the 2–3s group who had language delay and we were very pleased that the signing seemed to be helping them also.

About this time, however, we noticed that Margaret was not quite as forthcoming as usual and seemed a little anxious. Previously we had been working in a true partnership, sharing ideas and problems and we wondered what had brought about this slight, but noticeable change. This was our first real 'blip' in working with Christina and implementing our special needs policy. The Head and the SENCO had informal discussions with Margaret and discovered that she was concerned that by signing with her we would not use speech at all and that therefore Christina's speech would not be developed. This had been noted by Lorenz (1988: 35): 'Some parents still hold largely unfounded beliefs that signing will delay speech development. Others fear that signing will make their child "more handicapped"'. We assured Margaret that this would not happen and we think because of the trust that had developed between the centre and the family, Margaret's fears were allayed and she understood and accepted our strategy to use signing and speech simultaneously.

At all times we tried to keep Christina with her age group. Usually children are moved from the 0–2s room to the 2–3s room at age two and remain there until their third birthday. However we felt that Christina would benefit from an extra two months in the 0–2s room because of the more generous staff:children ratio, her particular needs at that time and because she was still only attending our centre for three days a week. We also delayed her move from the 2–3s room to the 3–5s room by two months. Apart from these occasions, Christina was always with children of her own age. We were aware that in the borough children were not usually statemented when in the Under Fives Education Centres. It seemed that the thinking was that children often make excellent progress when in the centres and therefore do not need statements. We felt that whatever progress Christina made with us, she was going to have Down's Syndrome all her life and would definitely need to have a statement at some time. We believed delaying a statement would not be in Christina's interests and could in fact hinder her progress. We met with some resistance initially but, through developing an excellent working relationship with the educational psychologist assigned to our centre, we were able to progress to Stage 4 of the assessment process. Again we noticed some resistance from Margaret, but this time we were not so surprised. Previously Christina's grandfather, who had telephoned to thank us for all the work we had put into supporting Christina, had telephoned the centre and said that the whole family was very grateful and extremely pleased with her progress. He told us that when Christina was born he had said, 'over my dead body will she go into mainstream education'. He said that he had felt very protective towards her and thought that in special education she would be more protected. He said, however, that he was later convinced by another family member, who strongly believed in inclusive education, that Christina should attend mainstream provision. The family had then decided to fiercely protect Christina's right to be in mainstream education and hence they chose Willow for her. When we consulted with the family about a statement for Christina, they had then wrongly (though not surprisingly) assumed that a 'statement' was the first step to separate special education and were therefore resistant to it. In support meetings with the family we explained that we saw the statementing process as a support for Christina and the family, that could in fact help her to remain in mainstream education.

The workers in the 3–5s room were very familiar with Christina before she transferred. At least one had experience of working with her in the toddler room, and all had many and varied contacts with Christina and her grandmother informally, as would be natural in a small closely knit centre. They also had much experience between them of working with and supporting children with special needs and their families. One had experience of working with Down's Syndrome children including one in her own family.

The general ethos in the centre was such that we were confident and comfortable in welcoming Christina into the room. We had as an underlying ethos the view that all children in our care must be treated as the individuals that they are, planned for and nurtured as such, and that we are co-workers with their families. We, of course, had our share of difficulties but we are committed to try to meet all our children's needs.

The structures involved in transition from the toddler room to the 3–5s room were set in operation. These were a meeting between the key worker in the toddlers, the new keyworker and Margaret. The workers relayed information about how the 3–5s room operated and asked Margaret for her view on how Christina was doing, her interests and how she was at home. This system was used also at all child support meetings between the keyworker, SENCO and the carers. Details of how the transition should be handled, Margaret's ideas on it, and her agreement and participation on the timetable of changing rooms was secured. This is as it would be for any child transferring. Christina, of course, had many informal visits into the room as had all the children transferring from the 2–3s room. Christina settled well into the room, although she liked to go into the 2–3s room for visits.

We had found that parents of children with an identified special need are anxious and often very vulnerable when the child is in the centre, but again this is an issue of trust and familiarity. It soon became clear that Christina's grandmother was very anxious that we did not underestimate Christina's potential and shared many examples of Christina's activities at home.

Margaret attended the regular child support meetings with the keyworker and SENCO to review the child's progress by focussing on her strengths and newly acquired skills. Areas of concern are agreed and targets are set to positively support the child. It is agreed at these meetings at which stage of the SEN *Code of Practice* the child should be recorded. However, from our point of view some of the best work was informal chatting at the end of the day, showing Christina's pictures and work to her grandmother and general discussions about her progress; this brought the discussion to the particular and with examples of work Christina had done and photographs of activities she was involved with, trust was being established. Both formal and informal contacts were important in supporting Christina

As with any child, work samples and photographs were kept over her time in the room and observations were fed into her individual planning and room planning. The structure and layout of the room and outside environment are ordered to allow the children maximum choice in activity (everything on the child's physical level). We encourage autonomy, negotiation and responsibility, all of which were as important to Christina as any other child, and she took advantage of this. The extra adult in the room did not follow Christina about; all adults worked with her, enabling, offering language, supporting her if necessary.

Through the observations kept on Christina and all the children, we would discuss in our weekly room meetings issues that had arisen or opportunities that needed to be given. For example, it was clear at one point that Christina was not coping too well with large story groups and steps were taken to support her in this activity, such as giving her the job of handing out the fruit before the story, showing her pictures to the whole group or choosing the story. Or, during her early time in the room she had a lot of wet clothes due to her love of water play and not getting to the toilet. This meant we had to work closely with Margaret, explaining to her that Christina enjoyed getting changed and that when she had wet knickers it didn't mean we didn't believe Margaret when she told us that she was dry at home. We explained that it was something we had seen before when children transferred rooms and we were quite happy to take Christina on trips to the laundry to try on our spare clothes even if her clothes were not wet. Having an extra adult in the room helped us to support Christina at these times as well as being able to offer more small group work to Christina, not only with stories and games but also planned activities that encouraged specific skills and learning intentions that we had identified. We could also offer more support to Christina in specific ways as the need arose, for example a trip to the shops, support in larger story groups, or help at tidying up times for Christina to do her share: never was the person used to follow Christina about or do things for her. The adult helped Christina to do things herself. There was sensitive intervention where necessary or specifically where an opportunity to further her learning had been seen. Christina was very used to doing lots of stimulating activities with her grandmother and we wanted to encourage and widen her confidence in interaction with others.

By the usual practice of observation Christina's interests and abilities were taken into account by the room staff and, after discussion with her grandmother, were incorporated into our planning. An earlier observation, made in the 2–3 year-olds room when she was settling in, noted that she was very independent, took off her nappy and sat herself on the potty. It was also noted that she liked lots of messy activities such as painting; that she drew everywhere, loved playing with dolls and prams, dressing up and water play. At that stage they noted she could say 'egg', 'drink juice', 'I want', 'no', 'yes' and 'baby'. Her interests which were noted by the staff in their observations in the 3–5s room included dressing up, drawing, painting, water play, computer, dolls, home corner, taking off and putting on her own shoes, songs with actions, her home and family, trips to the shops, chanting numbers and small group times.

At this point we also felt that she needed to be encouraged to participate confidently in larger groups, and to speak louder and that we needed to extend and recognise her language development. We needed to constantly ensure that we were taking into account her grandmother's concern that she should not be underestimated. For example, the use of topic planning provided good opportunities to support Christina's and all children's learning. Christina participated actively in accessing the topic of 'shoes' which was planned for the whole group under curriculum headings of mathematics, language and literacy, personal and social, physical, knowledge and understanding of the world (including science and technology), and creative and aesthetic. In the planning for mathematics, for example, Christina was able to join in the setting up of a shoe shop, with shoes and boxes, money and a cash till (including a credit card facility): this encouraged her mathematical language. She said, 'it didn't fit' when trying on different shoes, used colour names, sizes, etc., and had experience of matching pairs. She was motivated to join in the song about 'Baby shoes, Giant shoes' which supported the development of her size discrimination and she was able to draw around her own shoes. The extra support enabled these experiences to be particularly supported and followed up in small group working.

The information-gathering period early in Christina's time at the centre was crucial to our planning and setting of targets. The information we gathered then, together with observations of Christina at the centre, were used to set the first targets by the family, keyworkers and the SENCO. These targets focussed on supporting her balance and walking as well as modelling actions with language and encouraging attention to activities. In the following term we were then familiar with the *Code of Practice* and recognised that Christina was on Stage 3 of the Special Educational Needs *Code of Practice*. We were working with our learning support teacher, with the family's consent, and he spoke to her carers as well as the keyworker and SENCO. Sometimes he would attend a group room meeting to share information with the staff in the room. We had been setting targets in liaison with her carers, keyworker, SENCO and other specialists from her first term with us and we continued these termly meetings until she left for school.

Initially we were supporting her attempts to walk, with a lot of praise and encouragement, as well as giving her experience with the names of objects including the use of picture cards, objects and Makaton signs. At this time, a trainee educational psychologist did some work with Christina, and her recommendations were shared at meetings with her grandmother, our learning support teacher, our educational psychologist, the keyworker and SENCO. A programme of Makaton was decided on: new words would be introduced each week at home and at Willow to build on Christina's baseline knowledge of Makaton words.

The focus on Makaton resulted in a great interest among staff and some training for one group of staff. The following term Christina moved into the 2–3s room. The specialist speech therapist visited monthly and observed Christina working with a small group of children. We considered her recommendations when targets were being set for the term. Funding for extra support had to be applied for on a termly basis. We ensured that we had resources recommended by the speech therapist, which included picture cards of everyday objects that could be used to accompany objects, and Makaton signs. She also recommended that Makaton be used more in the larger group, which empowered it as another means of communication, which all the children benefitted from.

Transfer to school

Despite having started early, due to delays in the information gathering process, the information was not in place for the September when Christina was due to start school. During that period, however, both her grandmother and the SENCO were liaising with the school. The headteacher of the school said they would prefer to take Christina in when they had the support worker in place. Christina's grandmother and staff at Willow were pleased to continue their programmes of support until the assessment was through and the school was ready to offer extra support. The last term gave Christina a chance to be one of the oldest children in the room and she enjoyed helping the younger children.

We have learned from our work with Christina how the SEN *Code of Practice* can be implemented to support the child, and their family, as well as all the staff and professionals working together. It does demand a great deal of administration time and we are currently looking at ways of sharing this with all staff rather than relying as much on the SENCO. However, it is still essential that the SENCO has a coordinating role when there are so many people working together. The SENCO went on a borough-wide working party to develop Individual Education Plan proformas. We also learned that we may need to bring forward the timing for when we trigger the assessment process, as some of the early procedures can take longer than expected. The benefit of the delay meant that the family and the centre were able to liaise with Christina's school over her future support. It was agreed that the school would have a support worker in place for Christina's start date. Christina was familiar with the school as her relative attended, whom her grandmother also collected. The close liaison and cooperation, both formal and informal, in each transition stage helped to make her progress through an integrated centre into mainstream school a success. We are aware that all children with Down's Syndrome may not be offered such a choice of provision. However, we feel that high expectations and integrated opportunities have had a positive effect on Christina's education, and on her life.

Christina's presence had a positive effect on the development of the staff and the centre, and she was a joy to work with. We all learnt from the experience of working with her – perhaps we learnt more than she did.

References

Bird, G. and Buckley, S. (1993) *Meeting the Educational Needs of Children with Down's Syndrome: a Handbook for Teachers*, Portsmouth University: Sarah Duffen Centre.

DfEE (1994) *Code of Practice on the Identification and Assessment of Special Educational Needs*, London: HMSO.

—— (1997) *Excellence in Schools*, Green Paper, London: HMSO.

Miller, S. *et al.* (1991) *Vocabulary Acquisition in Young Children with Down's Syndrome: Speech and Sign*, abstract presented at 9th World Congress, Queensland: International Association of Scientific Study of Mental Deficiency.

Lorenz, S. (1998) *Children with Down's Syndrome*, London: David Fulton.

Chapter 4

Working with the young child who has special needs in the hospital setting

Pamela Barnes

One aspect of working with the child who has special needs, and one that is often overlooked, is in the hospital or health-care setting. Children with special needs and disability are more frequently admitted to hospital. This may be for treatment, surgery or simple observation. Now that play is recognized as an essential aspect of a child's treatment in hospital, it becomes important to offer appropriate opportunities for a child with special needs/disability to use play within health-care settings. This will require a level of expertise and special skills on behalf of the Hospital Play Specialist. The Hospital Play Specialist is now a fully recognized member of the multidisciplinary team and is trained to offer experiences of play for all children treated in health care settings.

Being admitted to hospital causes children and their parents considerable anxiety. Family life is shaken by the whole experience. Children who enter hospital will leave the security of their own home setting. They will be required to submit to various procedures, some will be painful and administered by strangers. Normal patterns of family life are abandoned for the time being. The prospect and reality of a stay in hospital can be a terrifying concept for a small child.

Nowadays professionals recognize the importance of understanding the needs of sick children when hospitalized. The Platt Report 'The Welfare of Children in Hospital' published in 1959 recommended that parents have continuous access to their child in hospital; that provision be made for them to stay; that those who care for sick children receive special training; and that children in hospital have opportunities for play recreation and continued education.

'The Welfare of Children and Young People in Hospital' published in 1991 by The Department of Health, takes into account all the developments in the care and treatment of children in hospital since the 1959 Platt Report. This new document recommends guidelines that comprise good practice and form the basis for clinical standards required for the health care of children and young people when they are suffering the effects of illness and hospitalization.

As play is an essential characteristic of childhood, and contributes to growth and development, it has now become an important element of treatment plans for children in hospital. Play in hospital assists coping strategies, thus reducing children's anxieties and offers the child a medium through which information can be given.

Deprived of play the child is a prisoner, shut off from all that makes life real and meaningful. Play is not merely a means of learning skills of daily living. The impulse to create and achieve, working through play, allows the child to grow in body and mind . . . Play is one of the ways in which children may develop a capacity to deal with the stresses and strains of life as they press upon them. It acts, too, as a safety valve, allowing them to play through and often come to terms with fears and anxieties which have become overwhelming.

(OMEP 1966)

In the Department of Health 1991 document, hospitals were advised, to 'provide play facilities in all areas of the hospital in which children are cared for' and to 'employ Hospital Play Specialists to fund play schemes' (Department of Health 1991: Section 4.12). Two further publications which contained advice and guidance on the provision of play in hospital were also recommended by The Department of Health: *Quality Management for Children: Play in Hospital*, published by Play in Hospital Liaison Committee, 1990 and the Save the Children Fund Publication, *Hospital: A Deprived Environment For Children? The Case For Hospital Playschemes* of 1989. These publications demonstrated that play was essential in supporting children in stressful situations such as an admission to hospital. Play has been found not only a welcome normalizing activity, but also to help to reduce anxiety, to facilitate communication and speed recovery and rehabilitation.

All children who are admitted to hospital share the same fundamental needs. The care provided by a hospital has to centre firmly on recognizing that the child is a member of a family and that the family will need appropriate support. Families need to be helped to become confident and competent in taking over the care of their child on discharge. This is extremely important where the child has an ongoing medical condition.

It is the responsibility of the NHS to provide services for children who need long term, perhaps indefinite health care. There should be local agreement with Social Services and Education to meet the needs of these children and their families. Health Action Zones have been initiated through government policy in order to address the issues of seamless boundaries; this being a priority in modernizing Health and Social Services (NHS 1998). The needs of the carers/families, a variety of respite care and support in black and ethnic families should also be addressed within this new format.

As a member of the multidisciplinary team in a paediatric unit, the Hospital Play Specialist will work alongside other professionals in order to see that all the children admitted to the unit will receive appropriate care, so that when a child who has special needs is admitted to hospital, they too will require the support given as to any sick child. When a child with a special need or a disability is admitted to hospital they can be doubly disadvantaged. It is essential for hospital personnel to ensure that facilities, procedures and staff understand the needs of these children and their families. Children with sensory impairments can be at risk of isolation alongside deprivation of information. Training will be required for all staff in order to understand the special needs of these children. Staff will also require a knowledge and understanding of the wide range of special educational needs. In the training of the Hospital Play Specialist this is an important curriculum area. The training takes into account the needs of blind/visually impaired children, deaf/hearing impaired, deaf/blind and multiply disabled children as well as children with physical and mental disability. Hospital Play Specialists are encouraged to liaise with the parents, the community facilities and the child's school, if appropriate, in order to become informed as to how they may be encouraged to help the child whilst in hospital. Many children do not bring into the hospital with them their specialized items of equipment. Without this equipment they may not be able to maintain their independence and continue to acquire new skills. Children with special needs and disabilities are children first and foremost and their disabilities should never detract from their needs and rights as children.

When entering hospital they should be admitted to paediatric wards where they will be nursed alongside non-disabled children. All treatment and procedures should be the same as those for non-disabled children within comparable circumstances. So the child with special needs or disability too needs the opportunity to play. The vital functions of play in hospital will also benefit these children. The quality of a play experience will bring enjoyment and reduce anxiety and stress in the immediate present. Play will help prevent developmental regression which could be vital for the child with special needs. Parents find that play experiences with their child in hospital provide a normalizing situation: this empowers them in regaining their parental role. As with able children, play improves the recovery rate and in skilled preparation sessions the Hospital Play Specialist can communicate some understanding of treatment and procedures to the child and his/her family. Many hospital staff may be unfamiliar with the physical care and management needs of children with multiple disabilities and do not have the special skills required to help these children. There can also be a lack of appropriate adaptive equipment available, yet the child may require many further admissions. For many parents caring for their child with special needs at home, a hospital admission can often be a 'final straw', particularly when returning home with a recovering disabled child still requiring nursing. The pressures on the family at this time can be almost unbearable. There is often parental depression and sometimes even family breakdown.

Admitting a child with a disability to a busy paediatric ward requires careful planning. Not only are there acute medical needs requiring immediate attention, but so too must all other needs be addressed.

Families who have a child with special needs will already have been in contact with many professionals. The children may even have to be seen by a number of consultants and often the referring GP, once having referred the child, leaves the care to the hospital. There is a very wide variation in referral practice, as in the treatment and care given prior to admission. Care plans should be drawn up in partnership with the child, parents and multidisciplinary team, the Hospital Play Specialist being a member of the latter. Children with learning and physical disabilities should also be involved in their care plans and their care plans will include play programmes. In fact, play with a child who has special needs may be the only effective tool of communication.

With the particular knowledge obtained through their training, a Hospital Play Specialist can contribute to the comfort and wider well-being of such a child. Play can be used to facilitate a more enlightened approach to the understanding of a child with special needs in a health-care setting. It is so important that the Play Specialist, the Nurse and Carer have the understanding, knowledge and training in order to be fully aware of each child and family's individual needs, their abilities, strengths, limitations and expectations. Only then can suitable play and stimulation be provided. Many families and children will need encouragement to play and develop new skills. Play should enable the child to enjoy suitable activities and to be able to have a positive experience. Although they may appear elusive, each child will have his or her strengths. The Carer, or Play Specialist requires understanding, patience and positive communication skills in order to find these strengths. Only then can help, support, and encouragement be offered. Every play experience should not only be positive but it should be pleasurable, satisfying and fun.

A wide range of play materials and equipment are necessary to cater for all needs, abilities and developmental levels. A wide variety will help the children have real choices, the focus is always on the ability rather than the disability. The Play Specialist will ensure that every child is enabled to participate to their full potential and make sure that no one is excluded from an activity in which they wish to participate. There should be no segregation of children with disability from able children. Particularly in a hospital situation, a child may need one-to-one attention. This will need to be programmed into the play timetable for the day, as play must continue to be a priority for the child with disability.

Handling of children is important, particularly for the child with multiple disabilities. Unless the child is positioned correctly, made to feel secure and given appropriate equipment he/she may not be able to play. This poses difficulties for the Hospital Play Specialist with a limited budget. Equipment that is adapted to meet the needs of a child with special needs is usually expensive. A good basic collection of toys to meet the needs of the child with disability is of great importance. However, there may be a toy library within reasonable distance of the unit and toys can be borrowed for the duration of the child's hospital admission. This often allows for the variety needed to widen the experiences offered to the child. The concept of using a toy library may also be introduced to the parents. Some hospitals are able to offer the services of their own toy libraries. This is more common within a Children's Hospital.

The Hospital Play Specialist will need not only to build up a good relationship with the child but also with his/her parents. This will support the family, and make for a feeling of security. Being asked to 'play' with their child is not usually enough. Parents, particularly in hospital may need specific guidelines. Helping to organize play in a planned way, and tailored to meet the child's needs, adds to the well-being of the working relationships.

Helping parents and others to use this opportunity to play is indeed helping this child to recover. The immobile child can often miss out on opportunities to play and explore unless their needs are understood. All children can play, but it will be at a level appropriate to their stage of development. This needs the ability of the facilitator to recognise these stages and build on current ability. As much of the parenting role has been handed over to the caring staff, the Play Specialist too needs to encourage parents to develop their own role through play and activities. An accurate observation of the level of ability is therefore of great importance in order to bring parents onboard as equal partners. Not only will the Play Specialist work alongside parents, but also alongside other members of the paediatric team. This will add to the depth of knowledge and understanding of the child and his/her illness. Working with the physiotherapist, speech therapist and dietitian when offering play opportunities to children with disability is help-ful with positioning, seating, necessary equipment and language stimulation.

A mutual understanding between nurses, doctors and play staff as to the role of play in supporting the sick child in hospital is also important. Nurses often have only brief opportunities for play, but are more likely to participate when a child is engaged in an organized activity. Doctors find that observations made through play enhance the clinical picture. Observations from the Hospital Play Specialist are often used in collecting information in case conferences when discussing the issue of 'statementing'.

In providing play for the child with special needs, all aspects of the child's needs and abilities must be taken into account. Perhaps most important, will be the likes and dislikes of the child and his/her family. The Play Specialist will need to know how to handle the child in order to offer maximum comfort, security and familiarity. The positioning of the child is also very important in helping the child achieve satisfaction and enjoyment without frustration. Perhaps the child will have favourite activities, such as music, water paint or relaxation within the multi-sensory room. Multi-sensory rooms are indeed a very positive way of helping a child to cope with a hospital experience and are now widely used. Liaison with the child's nursery or school or relevant organisation is also a helpful way of building up a more comprehensive picture. This allows for the opportunity of continuity in programmes, aiding positive play experiences, encouraging development of skills and aiming to develop new skills that will be able to continue after discharge.

Another area of play that can be encouraged encompasses tactile experiences. Not only can many creative materials be used, but many Hospital Play Specialists also use pets. Just stroking the pet rabbit has real therapeutic qualities and is of great benefit for a child who has little opportunity to be close to an adult or who has limited mobility.

As the process of play is far more important than either the toy or the end result, activities that incorporate tactile experiences are greatly valued in working in this area of disability. To obtain full benefit from a play session, the adult's attention needs to be undivided. Planning the environment in which play can be carried out will enhance the activity. The toys or materials will need to be presented in a way that will impose some discipline on the child, yet help him/her to concentrate on the activity in hand.

Many games and activities can be set up by the Hospital Play Specialist with particular goals in mind. It may be necessary to encourage the child with special needs to move, to encourage interest in food and eating, or even to explain fluid restriction. Activities that encourage interest in food could be 'group meals' for special diets, meals the children may have helped to cook, 'aroma/therapy and many others. A balance of activities is required; non-directed activities that the child and his/her family can enjoy just for the sake of enjoyment and being together, as well as directed play activities with particular therapeutic goals. So the play activities and materials that the Play Specialist will use can be grouped into the following categories:

- play for providing information
- play to encourage normalization
- play to use familial and other support systems
- play to help identify coping techniques.

The Hospital Play Specialist therefore has a very complex role and he/she must ever be mindful of cultural and other familial variables, yet not forget the maintenance of a safe environment and the safe use of materials. It is also important to remember that a child with special needs may require extra time and supervision with their play activities.

The careful selection of toys for therapeutic activities is of great importance and the Hospital Play Specialist may not have the storage space or resources in order to give as wide a variety of play as possible. Fortunately, there are now several organizations that will support the work of the Hospital Play Specialist, and the Special Needs pack available from Play Matters, The National Toy Libraries Association, is a very valuable resource, alongside Community Toy Libraries as previously discussed.

The Royal National Institute for the Blind offers very comprehensive advice and resources for helping children with visual impairment, and these are particularly useful for the Hospital Play Specialist when offering play opportunities in a hospital setting. The National Deaf Children's Society has issued guidelines for the care of children in hospital to help all staff who need to care for the child with a hearing impairment. The 'Planet Information Service' is also available and offers a wide range of support and advice. All the above are most useful in supporting Hospital Play Programmes.

In order to facilitate play for children with special needs in a health-care setting, training knowledge and understanding will be required. As previously stated, this is addressed in the training of Hospital Play Specialists. During their training, students' attention is drawn to various important documents pertaining to childrens' needs and rights. This will include important aspects of the Warnock Report (1978), the Education Act (1981), the Children Act (1989) and the *Code of Practice* (DfEE 1994). The Hospital Play Specialist may be called upon for their input into the way forward with a particular child. In order to be able to make a comprehensive contribution, a working knowledge of government documentation is essential. With the current philosophy of parental partnership alongside community education, the hospital perspective when treating a child who is suffering from illness and is at the same time disabled can be of great significance. The Hospital Play Specialist has a role to play in:

- Noting and sharing concerns
- Referral
- Assessment
- Action and intervention
- Recording
- Review

The Hospital Play Specialist may even be involved in devising goal plans and the setting out of a timetable for achieving short and longer term goals.

Training of Hospital Play Specialists has been offered as a qualification since 1988, in Colleges of Higher and Further Education. The Hospital Play Staff Education Trust (HPSET) who initiated the qualification is now the registration body, as EDEXCEL now offers the academic award. Both organizations work closely together in order to monitor the qualification, training and registration of Hospital Play Specialists. The qualification was recognised by the Department of Health and the Department of Education in 1992. At this time Hospital Play Specialists were recognised as a professional category of staff within the National Health Service. Further courses which have been developed jointly by HPSET and EDEXCEL are:

1   Professional Development Units in Updating Hospital Play Specialism
2   Professional Development Diploma in Hospital Play.

The Professional Development Diploma has a Unit of Study 'Disability and Learning Difficulty', which aims to enable the student to extend their current knowledge and understanding of children with disability and learning difficulties, over and above their current level of understanding.

The role of Hospital Play Specialists is developing and continues to do so. Not only do they offer an invaluable role within the busy paediatric ward, but recently they have joined community teams working with sick children in their own homes. This will of course include children with special needs and disability.

The caseload for a Hospital Play Specialist in the community will be a mixture of children who have special needs and chronic or life-threatening illness. Here

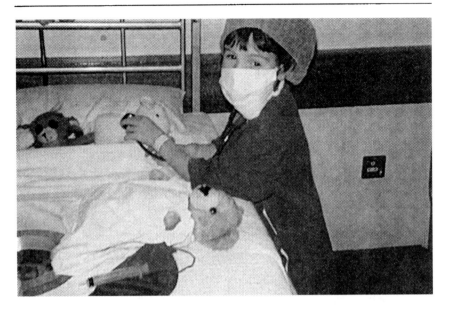

Figure 4.1 Play can be used as an aid to recovery and also for information

the role of the Hospital Play Specialist will extend into developing programmes of supportive activities for the siblings, often a forgotten group. The Hospital Play Specialist will have had the opportunity to observe a child prior to treatment, during treatment in hospital if required, and again on returning home. Of course the Hospital Play Specialist will be fully aware of professional boundaries and yet be able to share information through being a member of a Children's Community Nursing Team. Further training in counselling is essential and is also a unit of study available within the Professional Development Diploma.

The days of the child with special needs who is sick, admitted to hospital and isolated because of his/her inability to play, should be a thing of the past. With the knowledge, understanding and training received by Hospital Play Specialists, they can facilitate play to include all children who are sick at home or in hospital in using play as an aid to recovery. Children with special needs who are admitted to hospital are sick, just as other children who are admitted to hospital. They too deserve opportunities to play in order to enable and aid recovery.

Appendix: useful addresses

Action for Sick Children
300 Kingston Road
Wimbledon
London SW20 8LX

E.J. Arnold & Son Ltd (Suppliers)
Parkside Lane
Dewsbury Road
Leeds LS11 5TD

Community Playthings & Rifton
Robertsbridge
East Sussex TN32 5DR

Disabled Living Foundation
380–384 Harrow Road
London W9 2HV

Edu-Play Toys
Stephen Lenton & Corrina Orencas
10 Vestry Street
Leicester LE1 1WQ

James Galt & Co. Ltd (Suppliers)
Brookfield Road
Cheadle
Cheshire SK8 2PM

The Health Promotion Research Trust
49/53 Regent Street
Cambridge CN2 1AB

MENCAP
123 Golden Lane
London EC1Y 0RT

The Muscular Dystrophy Group of Great
  Britain
35 Macauley Road
London SW4 0QP

National Childrens' Bureau
8 Wakeley Street
London EC1 V7QE
National Deaf Childrens Society
45 Hereford Road
London W2 5AH

Nottingham Educational Supplies Ltd
17 Ludlow Hill Road
West Bridgford
Nottingham NG2 6HD

Planet Information Service
Cambridge House
Cambridge Grove
London W6 0LE

Play for Life
1–31B Ispwich Road
Norwich NR2 2LN

Play Matters
The National Toy Libraries Association
68 Churchway
London NW1 1LT

Rompa
PO Box 5
Wheatbridge Road
Chesterfield
Derbyshire S20 2AE
Royal Institute for the Blind
224 Great Portland Street
London W1N 6AA

Scope
12 Park Crescent
London W1N 4EQ

Sense – National Deaf/Blind & Rubella
  Association
311 Gray's Inn Road
London WC1X 8PT

Toys for the Handicapped
76 Barracks Road
Sandy Lane Industrial Estate
Stourport-on-Severn
DY13 9QB

Voluntary Council for Handicapped
  Children
c/o National Children's Bureau
8 Wakeley Street
London EC1V 7QE

Further reading

Action for Sick Children (1996) 'Special Needs Children in Hospital' London: Cascade.

Association for Teachers & Lecturers (1994) Achievement for All, London.

Astell-Burt, C. (1981) Puppetry for Mentally Handicapped People, Human Horizons Series, London: Souvenir Press.

BTEC/ED EXCEL (1997) Professional Development Diploma in Hospital Play Specialism.

Carr, J. (1985) Helping Your Handicapped Child, Middlesex: Penguin.

Children Act (1989) London: HMSO.

Department for Education and Employment (1978) Meeting Special Educational Needs, London: HMSO.

—— (1994) Code of Practice, London: HMSO.

Department of Health (1959) The Welfare of Children in Hospital – The Platt Report, London: HMSO.

—— (1991) Welfare of Children and Young People in Hospital, London: HMSO.

Edwards, M. and Davis, H. (1997) Counselling Children with Chronic Medical Conditions, Leicester: British Psychological Society.

Einon, D. (1985) Creative Play, Middlesex: Penguin.

Hart, R. Mather, P. Slack, J. and Powell, M. (1992) Therapeutic Play Activities in Hospitalized Children, London: Mosby Year Book.

Hogg, C. (1996) Health Services for Children and Young People, London: Action for Sick Children.

Hogg, C. and Rodin, J. (1990) Quality Management for Children, Play in Hospital, London: Play in Hospital Liaison Committee.

Jeffree, D. McConkey, R. and Hewson, S. (1977) Let Me Play, London: Souvenir Press.

Lansdown, R. (1980) More than Sympathy, London: Tavistock Publications.

—— (1996) Children in Hospital, Oxford: Oxford University Press.

Lear, R. (1990) More Play Helps, Oxford: Heinemann Medical.

Mitchell, D. (1982) Your Child is Different, London: George Allen & Unwin.

National Voluntary Council for Children's Play (1992) A Charter for All, London.

Newell, P. (1991) The UN Convention and Children's Rights in the UK, London: National Children's Bureau.

Newson, J. and Newson, E. (1979) Toys and Playthings, Middlesex: Penguin.

NHS Executive (1996) Child Health in the Community, A Guide to Good Practice, London: Department of Health.

NHS (1998) National Priorities Guidance 1999/2000 – 2001/2002, London: Department of Health.

O'Hagan, M. and Smith, M. (1993) Special Issues in Child Care, London: Bailliere Tindall.

OMEP (1996) Play in Hospital, World Health Organisation for Early Education.

Sandow, S. (1994) Whose Special Need, London: Paul Chapman Publishers.

Save the Children (1989) Hospital; A Deprived Environment for Children? The Case for Hospital Play Schemes: London.

Scott, E. James J. and Freeman, R. (1977) Can't Your Child See? Baltimore, MD: University Park Press.

Sutherland, A. and Soames, P. (1984) Adventure Play with Handicapped Children, Human Horizons Series, London: Souvenir Press.

Sylva, K. and Lunt, I. (1982) Child Development, Oxford: Basil Blackwell.

Tansley, P. and Panckhurst, M. (1982) Children with Specific Learning Difficulties, Windsor: NFER-Nelson.

Wolfson, R. (1989) Understanding Your Child, London: Faber and Faber.

Chapter 5

'Listen Hear'

Parents supporting parents with deaf children

Joy Jarvis and Karen Riley

'Hello Everyone! How are you?
Hello Everyone! How are you?
Hello Everyone! How are you?
How are you today?'

Eight mothers and eight children between the ages of one and four join in the song. They then sit and identify photographs of each child in the group and say hello to each other. They watch as a face of a child is built up on a felt board. The eyes, the nose, the mouth, the ears, the hearing aids. Then they all join in Grandmother's footsteps, Five Little Ducks and Row the Boat, all with actions. Then it's time for a story from a pop-up book. A 'What's in the box?' activity is followed by cutting and sticking. Soon all the children are wearing paper hats. They play together while their Mums drink coffee and chat. Then it's time to tidy up and go home. Some will face a journey of over an hour to get home. They will be back again next Thursday. Why do they come?

This chapter will explore how and why parents of young deaf children developed their own group to support each other and to foster the language development of their children. It looks at how they researched sources of information for ideas for structures and activities, and how they liaised with professionals in the field. Implications for good practice in parent–professional partnerships are highlighted.

The 'Listen Hear' group

'I come to the "Listen Hear" group so he can see other children with hearing aids; so he knows he's not the only one.' 'I bring her because the activities are at her level.' 'I come to meet other people in the same boat and get ideas from them.' Parents identify the need for their children to meet other deaf children and to begin to develop their identity and self-esteem. They identify their own need to find out how other families are dealing with bringing up a deaf child in a hearing family. They also see that their child has difficulty joining in many of the activities at the local play group. The stories and songs are too difficult for children who are only using a few words or signs to understand. Also the parents want the children to learn listening and communication skills. In the 'Listen Hear' group key words and concepts are identified and developed. 'Open' is used when a box is opened to find out what's inside, when the door is opened, when the biscuit tin is opened. Parents talk about how they can use this word or sign at home; open the fridge, open the window, open the tin of beans. Supporting their deaf child's development of communication skills will be a central concern for these parents for years to come and they are identifying the need for support to do this.

Starting the group

The support in this case is coming from other parents. This group is organised and run by three mothers. They have developed the group from a few people meeting in a front room through a number of locations of varying suitability to their present venue in a room in a health centre where the audiology clinic is also located. The three mothers have found sources of funding from the early-years department of the social services and from national and local charitable organisations. They have advertised for members in the local paper, through notices in doctors' waiting rooms, through the newsletter of the local voluntary deaf children's society. Teachers of the deaf employed by the local education authority and audiologists employed by the local health trusts recommend the group to parents of newly diagnosed deaf children.

Looking for ideas

In order to find out about bringing up deaf children and the activities they wanted to do in the 'Listen Hear' group, the parents actively sought information from a range of sources. These included what could be seen as the traditional suppliers of this information to parents of deaf children: professionals employed as teachers of the deaf, speech and language therapists and audiologists in the education and health services. They also looked at a range of books and at materials produced by voluntary and charitable organisations working in the field. They visited other parent-led groups and attended courses. What they found was that much of the material available in the field is biased. This is partly due to the continuing controversy about whether to develop oral or signed communication. The role of British Sign Language as a potential first language for deaf children has become more significant during the past ten years, while at the same time improved technology is bringing the possibility of hearing to deafer children. This includes the use of cochlear implants, whereby electrodes are inserted into the inner ear to stimulate the auditory nerve, which can give profoundly deaf children access to sound. While some see this as opening the door of the hearing world to deaf children, others see it as a medical response to a cultural difference and the denial of a deaf child's right to be deaf and to use an alternative, signed, language. Material parents find, and people they talk to, will have different perspectives on these issues.

As has been noted by researchers in the field, many sources of information will give one side of an argument and may not even indicate that there is a different view (Beazley and Moore 1995). As parents will have to make decisions on a number of issues fairly quickly, due to the importance of the early years for learning language, they need to be able to access a range of opinions. They need to act as consumers (Cunningham and Davis 1985) and to look for the advice and services they want. In the case of the 'Listen Hear' parents they were able to do this effectively. In one case, for example, the parents attended a course run by a group advocating developing deaf children's listening and talking, even though sign language was already being used with the child at home. 'It was a really good course with lots of ideas. We pretended we didn't sign' said a parent. It would seem unfortunate that parents may feel they have to hide their opinions in order to access information when they need to be able to explore all avenues and views.

Professional support for 'Listen Hear'

The three mothers also asked a number of different professionals in the field of deaf education to visit the 'Listen Hear' group and give advice about the activities and how they were being done. This included the advisory teachers for pre-school deaf children who were employed by the LEA and whose main job was to make home visits to the families of deaf children. The advisory teachers arranged to visit the group regularly to give advice. These teachers were not the only source of advice, however, and again the parents could be seen as acting as consumers in seeking a range of different sources for their ideas. They were also, of course, acting as service providers as they were providing a service for deaf children and their families; a type of provision that was not currently being provided by the professional service providers. Carpenter, looking at current developments in working with families with children with special educational needs, notes that good practice can be seen when families are not only receiving services, 'but were also seen as service deliverers themselves' (1997: 24). In the case of 'Listen Hear' the service provided by the parents was not set up as part of a planned parent–professional partnership but came about because three parents felt that there was a need for a service currently not being provided. Professionals, however, were happy to support the parents and gave time to helping them to find rooms, recommending other families to attend the group, and offering advice on suitable activities and approaches to developing communication skills.

'Listen Hear' moves on

As they come up to the second anniversary of starting 'Listen Hear', the parents feel that the group is evolving and that the three leaders are beginning to empower other parents within the group. They are now sharing and negotiating the content of the sessions with the parents who attend, and encouraging them to take responsibility for a particular session, such as the story or an action song. They are also all discussing together the future of the group. Initially the focus was on listening and on using voice. Now a number of parents are also looking for support for sign communication so it has been agreed to build up a vocabulary of useful signs which will be used during group activities. The three leaders feel that the more parents are involved in running the group the more likely they are to continue to attend. Also the parents are more likely to grow in confidence and feel that they can make decisions. One could argue that this could lead to parents having greater confidence in their ability to influence provision.

Parent–professional partnership

Developing a partnership between parents and professionals can be seen as one of the key issues in special educational needs during the past decade. The importance of parents in the education of their children and their right to be part of the decision-making process has been recognised and enshrined in legislation and practice. Professionals are expected to work with, and not just for, families. Numerous publications have been produced for professionals to help them to work more effectively with parents (Gascoigne 1995; Blamires, Robertson and Blamires 1997; Wolfendale 1997). Groups and advice centres such as the Independent Panel for Special Education Advice (IPSEA) offer help and support for parents in working with professionals and understanding their rights and procedures. At times professional–parent relationships can become fraught with difficulty, however this is often because professionals are working within structural and budgetary limitations which conflict with the hopes and expectations that parents have for provision. The result can be conflict and the use of the special needs tribunal to adjudicate (Dale 1996).

Issues for teachers of the deaf

Partnership with parents and early intervention in relation to children with special needs is advocated in the SEN *Programme of Action* (DfEE 1998) but how are parents and professionals currently working together to meet the needs of the family and the young deaf child? As Dale (1996) notes, there are many different concepts of partnership. The notion of the professional as the expert with all the knowledge and skills was largely replaced during the 1970s by the 'transplant relationship' in which the professional recognised that parents had an important role to play in the development of the young child and aimed to give them some of the professional skills, such as communicating with deaf children, to enable them to be the child's teachers. In relation to teachers of the deaf, the change in practice was from visiting children at home and giving demonstration lessons, which the parent would be expected to repeat during the period before the next visit, to offering advice regarding parents' interaction with their children. The practice of videotaping parents interacting with their children and then analysing the footage together, has been advocated as an appropriate way of encouraging parents to continue with strategies they are using effectively and to encourage the development of new approaches (Cole 1992; Stokes 1994).

Parents in the 'Listen Hear' project were keen for professionals to give ideas and practical strategies for communication. They also liked to observe professionals interacting with individual children so that they could pick up ideas. They felt that they could generally adapt ideas and incorporate them into their own interaction styles. They also felt that if they understood the reason behind a particular strategy they could generalise it into their own context. This may not be the case for all parents. How a range of parents can be helped to develop their own appropriate communication with their deaf child is one of the key issues for teachers of the deaf. Teachers working in schools often report that a particular child is only able to communicate at school, and interviews with deaf young people suggest that many have real difficulties communicating within their families (Gregory 1995). This suggests that a clear focus for professionals must be on supporting families with communication. But how can this be done?

How can communication be supported?

It is clear that the parents' skill in interacting with their deaf child can have a considerable effect on that child's development of language and communication (Harris 1992; Gallaway and Woll 1994). It is perhaps less clear how parents can be supported in their development of communication that is appropriate for their child and family. Kelman and Schneider (1994) undertook a project with parents of pre-school, hearing children with language difficulties. In addition to individual sessions in which a parent and professional would view video tapes of the parent interacting with their child and discuss effective strategies, parents attended a course in which aspects of language such as turn-taking, attention and play were explained and discussed. The third strand to the intervention was a series of sessions for the group of children run by speech and language therapists. The parents viewed these sessions via a TV monitor and undertook observation activities which they discussed in the parents' group. In this way they had access to support with their individual skills which they were using with their child at that stage of development (and which of course would need to change as their child got older), they had opportunities to study language development and thereby learn the reasons behind using different strategies and they were also able to see these strategies modelled by professionals.

The authors report that the project was highly successful in terms of increased parent confidence and effectiveness in communicating with their child and in improved child language. It is likely that certain aspects of the programme were more suitable for different parents and that by using a range of approaches to learning they were able to support parents with different learning styles. As well as individual learning styles, cultural and socio-economic factors will affect how learning comes about. It is interesting to note that Kelman and Schneider found that 'parents from higher socioeconomic groups generally found it more difficult to accept, implement and maintain changes in their management and inter-action with their child' (1994: 93). If parents are to run the 'Listen Hear' group they need, not only to learn skills for interacting with deaf children, but also ways of sharing these with other parents. The parents running the group, all of whom are university educated, felt that if they were clear about the underlying objec-tives, they could generate ideas for practice themselves. This may not, of course, be the way that other parents attending the group learn best.

Recent changes in practice

Currently in the field of deaf education the area of most growth, in terms of professionals working with parents, is in relation to cochlear implant centres. These centres, generally located within medical provisions where the operations take place, employ teachers of the deaf and speech and language therapists to undertake 'rehabilitation' with children with implants. With young children this involves asking the parents to undertake a specific programme to develop their children's listening and language skills (Archbold and Robinson 1997). In many ways this could be seen as returning to more child-focused remediation rather than family-focused communication development. It could be that centre teachers and therapists are assuming that local teachers of the deaf will be working with parents on more general communication development, but this division of responsibility is by no means explicit (Archbold and Robinson 1997; Dryden 1997). Parents leading the 'Listen Hear' group felt that there was a security involved in working within a structured framework, provided the principles were clear so that they could incorporate targets into everyday living. They felt that the advice to 'let language develop naturally' was too vague and unhelpful when the child was able to access very little speech. They were looking for a balance between a structure for development, and support for their own individual skills. In order to change and develop their communication, however, parents need to take control and to have the confidence to make choices. This means that the professional working with parents of young deaf children cannot only concentrate on the issues of communication and amplification, however important these are (Watson and Lewis 1997). Parents need to be empowered to take control of their own situation.

Empowering parents

The transplant model of parent–professional working has a strong supportive role: it enables parents of young deaf children to further their knowledge and skills in communication development and to learn about and manage hearing aids and other audiological equipment; yet it is not a real partnership as most power lies in the hands of the professional. Dale (1997) notes that there has been a development in the 1980s and 1990s of more equal models of partnership. The parent as consumer has already been discussed in relation to the 'Listen Hear' group where parents made choices from a range of sources of information. The empowerment model argues that parents need to be empowered in order to choose and make decisions effectively in relation to which forms of service they require.

Certainly the parents running the 'Listen Hear' group felt that organising the group had empowered them. When asked if they would like professionals to take over the group, they responded that they would not, as they did not want to be 'swamped' by professionals. They wanted to have their own vision and control of the group, but they also wanted increased professional support for modelling activities and skills, for taking some sessions so that the children had trained professional input and for giving advice. When asked about improvements for the future, the parents talked about changes in location, having more appropriate rooms and a centre where parents and professionals could work together, rather than a change in the parent–professional relationship. This idea of having parents rather than professionals in the driving seat will be a very new concept for most teachers of the deaf who will generally have a background of working in schools. Forecki, a parent of a deaf child talks about her relationship with her child's first school. She is told to undertake certain activities at home because home support makes the school's job so much easier. 'Funny', she muses, 'I thought good schools made my job easier' (1985: 46). This relocation of power requires new skills on the part of professionals which in turn has training implications. Currently there are limited opportunities for training for teachers of the deaf working with families, and much of the support for these teachers comes from self-help groups. This is useful for sharing current knowledge but is perhaps not likely to generate new models of working.

What type of support?

The parents who run the 'Listen Hear' group see part of their role as supporting other parents in coming to terms with their child's difficulty, what Luterman (1987) calls the family 'making philosophical sense of the situation'. Many parents of deaf children and indeed parents of children with special needs generally, see parents as the best supporters of other parents. They have experience and can empathise with someone in a similar position to themselves. Parents setting up support groups for other parents is not unusual (Beazley and Moore 1995; Cashmore 1993; Luterman 1987). The 'Listen Hear' parents argue that parents will trust other parents, whereas they may feel that professionals have their own agendas and may have a vested interest in, for example, recommending a particular type of communication approach. Also, as a 'Listen Hear' parent observed recently, the professional does not live with the situation. Parents can also suggest ways of managing a range of practical situations, such as road safety, from their own experience. Families, of course, will not necessarily get on just because they both have a deaf child. Parents will not necessarily have skills to work with others. This, again, has implications for training. One could argue that, in a context of limited resources, it is the best use of professional time to help parents to gain the appropriate skills to provide support for other parents. Provided facilities such as rooms, transport and contacts were available, parents could run their own support groups. Information could also be provided for parents by other parents.

The 'Listen Hear' mothers are currently writing an information pack for other parents which includes accounts of their own children's diagnosis and the families' reaction to it; practical ideas for the management of hearing aids; ideas for communicating with very young deaf children; details of benefits and how to apply for them; an explanation of the role of the different professionals the family is likely to come into contact with, and a suggested reading list. The parents feel that all this information is not available in an easily accessible form and that they particularly valued reading about family experiences.

Autobiographies by parents are really appreciated but few parents will undertake this. Short accounts by local parents of their experience, however, can fairly easily be shared and a range a different families would ensure that not just one point of view is given. A suggestion by a parent interviewed by Beazley and Moore (1997) was to have videos showing the family and the deaf child and parents talking about their experiences. The parent felt that these could then be viewed at a convenient time for the family and additionally there was the potential for switching them off! While it might be difficult for a small support service to develop this type of resource, national groups for parents of deaf children may well be in a position to do this.

Towards inclusion?

Historically very young deaf children were sent to special schools, often boarding schools, on the grounds that only teachers of the deaf had the necessary skills to develop their pupils' communication and to support their learning. More recently, with a move towards local provision and inclusion, the majority of deaf children are educated in mainstream schools. Nevertheless, in some areas there is an emphasis on early education in a specialist environment. This is due partly to a concern about developing communication as early as possible and also to an increasing role for British Sign Language (BSL) in the education of some deaf children. As most parents will not be fluent users of sign language, there is the need for good models of the language from native BSL users. While deaf professionals will visit families at home, a number of areas provide 'deaf' playgroups and very early provision within resourced nursery settings where both deaf and hearing teachers, therapists and communicators can work with young children in a group context which will include both hearing and deaf children. (Knight 1997). In Newham, for example, it is anticipated that deaf children will be attending a nursery with additional resources for deaf children on a full time basis from the age of three (Robinson 1997). They may well be transported some distance from their home and so communication between home and school may not be easy. This early involvement of professionals working with deaf children is in line with the desire of the 'Listen Hear' parents to have teachers of the deaf working with their children in a group context. These professionals have the skills and experience to do this and possibly also fluency in BSL. However, there is a danger that, without ongoing family support in addition to the educational provision, the child's communication skills may be developed, but communication within the family and the parents' confidence may be diminished. The 'Listen Hear' parents felt that their own skills had improved immeasurably by having to be providers in their group context.

Where next?

Currently, a key issue being faced by providers of services for families of young deaf children is the possibility of universal neonatal hearing screening. It is possible for a baby to be identified with a hearing loss at a few days old. While this service is usually available for 'at risk' babies, in some areas it is available for all (Watkin and Nanor 1997). This results in an increasing number of families with very young deaf children being referred to the support services. This has implications for staffing and resourcing and for the development of new skills by the professionals involved. It is important that services develop with parents and not just for parents. A project such as 'Listen Hear' helps us to reflect not only on what type of services are being provided but also on how they are being provided. It suggests that those of us working as professionals in the field of special educational needs in the early years must consider how truly we work in partnership with parents.

The 'Listen Hear' parents highly value professional services but they would like to function in a context where they fully participate in setting the agenda. One could argue that they are not typical parents. However, all parents of deaf children have to make a number of decisions for their children and their family. They need to be empowered to do this effectively. Carpenter (1997) sees one way of doing this as supporting parents as researchers, whereby they observe, plan, take action and reflect on child and family needs before starting the cycle again. He argues: 'The days of professionals as expert have gone; what are needed now are informed supporters.' (1997: 29). In many ways the professionals supporting the Listen Hear' group could be seen as acting in this way. Services for families of young deaf children need to have both expertise in the field and structures and skills to enable them to work in real partnership with parents. A good start is to 'Listen Hear' to families.

Acknowledgements

The authors would like to thank Jane Savage and Rozanna Wright, the other founder members of 'Listen Hear'.

References

Archbold, S. and Robinson, K. (1997) 'Cochlear implantation, associated rehabilitation services and their educational implications', *Deafness and Education* 21(1): 34–41.

Beazley, S. and Moore, M. (1995) *Deaf Children, Their Families and Professionals*, London: David Fulton.

Blamires, M. Robertson, C. and Blamires, J. (1997) *Parent–Teacher Partnership: Practical Approaches to Meet Special Educational Needs*, London: David Fulton.

Carpenter, B. (ed.) (1997) *Families in Context: Emerging Trends in Family Support and Early Intervention*, London: David Fulton.

Cashmore, E. (1993) *Perceptions of Parent/Professional Relationships*, unpublished MA Dissertation, University of East Anglia.

Cole, E. (1992) *Listening and Talking: A Guide to Promoting Spoken Language in Young Hearing-Impaired Children*, Washington: Alexander Graham Bell Association for the Deaf.

Cunningham, C. and Davis, H. (1985) *Working with Families: Frameworks for Collaboration*, Milton Keynes: Open University.

Dale, N. (1996) *Working with Families of Children with Special Needs: Partnership and Practice*, London: Routledge.

DfEE (1998) *Special Educational Needs: A Programme of Action*, London: HMSO.

Dryden, R. (1997) 'A study of collaboration between the implant professionals and local educators in the rehabilitation of children with cochlear implants', *Deafness and Education* 21(2): 3–9.

Forecki, M (1985) *Speak to Me*, Washington: Gallaudet University Press.

Gallaway, C. and Woll, B. (1994) 'Interaction and Childhood Deafness' in C. Gallaway and B. Richards *Input and Interaction in Language Acquisition*, Cambridge: Cambridge University Press.

Gascoigne, E. (1995) *Working with Parents as Partners in SEN*, London: David Fulton.

Gregory, S. (1995) *Deaf Young People and Their Families: Developing Understanding*, Cambridge: Cambridge University Press.

Harris, M. (1992) *Language Experience and Early Language Development: From Input to Uptake*, Hove: Lawrence Erlbaum Associates.

Kelman, E. and Schneider, C. (1994) 'Parent–child interaction: an alternative approach to the management of children's language difficulties', *Child Language, Teaching and Therapy* 10(2): 81–95.

Knight, P. (1997) 'Bilingual nursery provision: a challenging start', *Deafness and Education* 21(3): 20–30.

Luterman, D. (1987) *Deafness in the Family*, Boston: Little, Brown & Co.

Robinson, M. (1997) 'Supporting Deaf Children in the Early Years' in Wolfendale, S. (ed.) *Meeting Special Needs in the Early Years: Directions in Policy and Practice*, London: David Fulton.

Stokes, J. (1994) 'The Use of Video-Tape in the Management of Young Hearing-Impaired Infants', *British Association of Teachers of the Deaf, Association Magazine*, Jan: 14–18.

Watkin, P. and Nanor, J. (1997) 'The implications for educational services of neonatal hearing screening', *Deafness and Education* 21(1): 19–33

Watson, L. and Lewis, S. (1997) 'Working with parents: setting the parameters', *Deafness and Education* 21(2): 32–40.

Wolfendale, S. (ed.) (1997) *Meeting Special Needs in the Early Years: Directions in Policy and Practice*, London: David Fulton.

Chapter 6

Research and practice

An evaluation of an education improvement strategy to support teachers and parents of young children with special educational needs

Jo Fieldhouse, Christine Pascal, Anthony Bertram and Sheila Gatiss

Introduction

This chapter describes and discusses a new education development programme trialled by a team of researchers, home teachers, managers, and parents of young children with special educational needs. The main aim of the programme was to adapt the Effective Early Learning Project (Pascal *et al.* 1996) and to assess its validity for use with home teachers and the families of young children with special educational needs within Essex Special Needs Support Service (SNSS). The Parent Partnership and Individual Child (PPIC) model was developed and then implemented by a home teaching team within the service. The process was audited to assess whether it had been an effective tool in improving the quality of service and enhancing the learning process for the teachers, parents and children involved in the study. The audit was predominately based upon the reported experiences of the parents and the teachers. Their voices proved significant and their experiences interlocked with theoretical perspectives on adult learning and self empowerment. The audit data has since been utilised to analyse the strengths and weaknesses of the model so that a further trial is tested and revised within a wider range of group settings appropriate for young children (between 2–4 years of age) with special educational needs. The two significant areas of development were the involvement of the parents working alongside the teachers to undertake observations and use the information collected and the adaptation of the EEL Project to focus upon the individual child.

Our thanks go to the partnership teams and children in Essex who have provided the data for this phase of the development and for their commitment and hard work.

The Effective Early Learning project and how the new PPIC process evolved

The main EEL Project began in May 1993. Its focus was in the provision for 3 and 4 year-olds who are currently in a wider range of provision than any other age group, but its methods and principles are applicable to any age. The project operates throughout the UK and is being carried out by a team of practitioner researchers, directed by Professor Christine Pascal and Dr Tony Bertram, based at the Centre for Research in Early Childhood, University College, Worcester.

An evaluative framework

The Pascal and Bertram Quality Evaluation Framework (see Pascal *et al.* 1996) builds upon the consensus about what constitutes quality in early childhood and also the knowledge base we have about effective early learning. The evaluative framework (represented diagrammatically in Figure 6.1) is based on quality indicators involving ten contextual dimensions and a developmental process involving detailed observations of practice. The framework takes participants

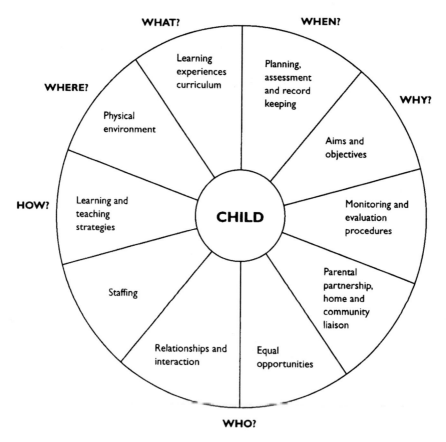

Figure 6.1 The Pascal and Bertram Quality Framework Design
Source: Pascal *et al.* 1996: 8

through a systematic and rigorous four-stage process of evaluation and development. This cycle takes approximately 12–18 months to complete.

Stage 1: Evaluation

The quality in relation to each of the ten contextual dimensions of quality is carefully documented and evaluated using a number of research methods in which all participants are fully trained. This involves a detailed quantitative and qualitative based assessment. Two key observation techniques measure the process, by looking at Child 'Involvement' and Adult 'Engagement'. These two techniques are central to both the main EEL Project and the newly developed PPIC model and so a brief summary of their content is outlined below.

CHILD INVOLVEMENT SCALE

This scale is an observation instrument developed by Laevers (1994), measuring a child's 'deep level learning'. Laevers suggests that a prime indicator of effective learning is associated with the levels of 'Involvement' a child is showing. He puts forward nine 'signals' of involvement (Laevers 1994) which include:

- concentration
- energy
- creativity
- facial expression and posture
- persistence
- precision
- reaction time
- language
- satisfaction

The observation is graded on a 1 to 5 level, level 1 being given when a child displays 'No Involvement' and level 5 being given when a child displays 'Intense Involvement'. Practitioners who have been involved in the EEL Project have found this scale very accessible and easy to use. It was therefore considered to have the potential to be adapted to meet the more specific needs of young children with special needs.

THE ADULT ENGAGEMENT SCALE

Within the main EEL Project, the Adult Engagement Scale (Laevers 1994; Bertram 1996) was designed to assess the quality of the adults' interaction with a group of children. This scale was based upon the belief that the quality of the interactions between the educator and the child is a critical factor in the effectiveness of the learning experience. The scale is on a continuum, graded on a point scale which reflects the degree to which the observed actions convey specific adult qualities. The observations focus on three areas:

(a) Sensitivity
This is the sensitivity of the adult to the feelings and emotional well-being of the child, involving elements of empathy, sincerity and authenticity. The observation focuses on the adults' responsiveness to a range of children's needs including the need for respect, attentiveness, security, affection and praise.

(b) Stimulation
This is the way the adult stimulates the child, introduces an activity and stimulates action.

(c) Autonomy
This is the degree of freedom the adult gives the child to experiment, make judgements, choose activities and express ideas.

The Parent Partnership and Individual Child Process

The PPIC model (see Figure 6.2) is an adaptation of the main EEL framework which has been developed to focus upon the individual child with special educational needs and their parents rather than upon a whole setting. It involves both the Child Involvement Scale, the Adult Engagement Scale and a new observational scale, the Parent Partnership Scale.

When the PPIC model was implemented, parents played a highly significant part. The Adult Engagement Scale was used by the parents to make observations of their child's home teacher whilst they were working with the child within the home. Originally, there was some apprehension about this task, but once both parties had used the scale it was found to be a useful and enlightening observational tool.

The new Parent Partnership Scale (see Appendix) was based upon the belief that the quality of support is dependent upon the relationship that develops between the parent and the practitioner. A team of managers from the Essex SNSS observed the teacher and the parent working together and in doing so completed the observation schedule. Again, this scale was a continuum based on a graded 5 point scale.

Stage 2: Action Planning

Participants met together to identify priorities for action based upon the evidence gathered from using the observation tools. This was a collaborative task which brought about real opportunities for active dialogue, equal participation and agreed strategies for future learning.

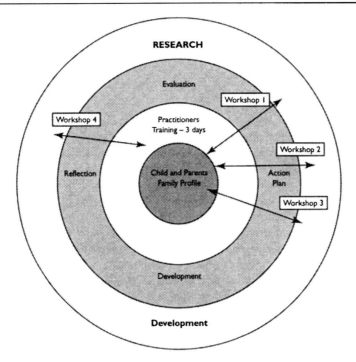

EEL PROCESS
Evaluation Phase
(a) *Quality Documentation*
- Context Proforma
- Documentary Analysis
- Photographs
- Physical Environment Schedule
- Professional Biographies
- Interviews with parents, teachers, managers
(b) *Quality Assessment*
- Child Involvement Scale
- Adult Engagement Scale
- Adult Partnership Scale

Action Phase
An Action Plan is developed with participants

Developmental Phase
Action Plan is implemented and the following observations are reapplied
Child Involvement Scale
Adult Engagement Scale

Reflection Phase
Monitoring and critical reflection of the impact of the improvement phase

LEARNING TOGETHER
Practitioners Induction Training
= three days

Workshop 1: Parents and practitioners
i) Introduction to Child Tracking, and Child Involvement Scale
ii) Practice

Workshop 2: Parents and practitioners
i) De-brief on Involvement Scales
ii) Introduction Adult Engagement Scale
iii) Practice

Workshop 3: Parents and practitioners
i) De-brief Adult Engagement
ii) Introduction Adult Partnership Scale
iii) Practice

Workshop 4:
i) De-brief on whole process
ii) Sharing and looking at Family Profiles
CELEBRATION

Figure 6.2 The EEL Parent Partnership and Individual Child Model
Source: Pascal *et al*. 1996: 25

Stage 3: Improvement

The Action Plan to improve the quality of provision was implemented, a process which took approximately six months.

Stage 4: Reflection

Participants were encouraged to reflect upon the evaluation and improvement process and to review the impact of the Action Plan. In order to identify whether any changes in relation to the child's involvement and to the levels of the adults engagement had occurred, the two key assessment schedules were re-implemented and then compared with that of the earlier data.

The process to develop and implement the PPIC model started at the beginning of 1996 in Essex. The overall objective was to look at how the main EEL tools for evaluating the quality of learning in a given setting could be adapted and used by an experienced team of home teachers working with parents of young children with a range of profound special needs.

There were two stages to the work undertaken. The first stage was to become familiar with the main EEL Project and to adapt it for use with an individual child with special educational needs. The second stage was to test the new materials and to comment on its effectiveness. This work proved to be a challenge. For the majority of the participants the process worked well and most learned a tremendous amount. For a few the process was arduous and the individual irritations experienced from the additional work had to be undertaken on top of pressured work loads. The enormous commitment and work done by all who participated, must be gratefully acknowledged. Teachers were pushed for time but worked diligently in their own time so that other children on their case loads did not suffer. Parents were open, honest and welcoming even though they were always under pressure trying to meet a variety of needs.

'Learning Together' workshops

Parents and teachers participated at the workshops to learn about the observational tools, to share their experiences of the process and to discuss whether the process had helped them in any way.

New strategies for working together focused upon the individual child. To summarise, the PPIC model differed from the main EEL process in a number of significant ways.

- Observations of the individual child were based on customised signals of 'Involvement' agreed collaboratively between the parents and the teachers. These signals were applied to a specific child rather than to a group of children.
- The focused and systemised observations of 'Involvement' were undertaken by the parents as well as by the teachers.

- The Adult Engagement Scale was used by the parents to observe the teacher and the child working together. It focused, in particular, on the sensitivity of the teacher to the child, the style of the teacher's stimulation and the degree of autonomy they encouraged.
- A new Parent Partnership Scale was developed and used to evaluate aspects of adult to adult interaction, specifically between the home teacher and the parent.
- Four 'Learning Together' workshops were held so that parents and teachers were learning together in a supportive and stimulating environment.
- Each teacher compiled a 'Family Profile' which comprised of data and photographs and reflected a snapshot of the learning process of the individual child over a period of ten months.

The audit – how did the PPIC process work in practice?

Conducting the audit

The aim of the audit was to gain a pragmatic and holistic insight into how useful the PPIC process had been as a vehicle to support teachers, and parents who had young children with special needs. The audit encompassed a mainly qualitative methodological approach which was formative and involved action research. The research was carried out in natural, 'real world' settings (Lincoln and Guba 1985; Robson 1995) which involved young children, parents and teachers working together in their familiar home environment.

A multi-method and multi-participant approach enabled the triangulation of mainly qualitative methods of data collection. Emphasis was placed upon triangulation to prevent an exclusive reliance on one method, to elucidate a variety of view points and to enhance accuracy and validity (Yin 1989).

Focused semi-structured interviews

Interviews proved to be a useful technique to capture the respondents' personal experiences of, and views about the effectiveness of the PPIC process. In order to achieve the research aims, it was important to find a way of enabling parents to speak honestly for themselves. Semi-structured interviews were considered to be a flexible and adaptable way of elucidating the parents' genuine reflections and rather analogous to a 'conversation with a purpose' (Robson 1995). Face-to-face interviews also offered support for the families, enabling the interviewer to rephrase the questions without changing the content.

The parents were interviewed twice, before the process began and once the process had been completed. They were asked to reflect upon the PPIC model and were invited to give constructive feedback. The parents were encouraged to keep diaries to enable them to make more accurate reflections upon the process.

Questionnaires

Questionnaires were circulated to the sixteen home teachers. All sixteen questionnaires were successfully completed and provided a wealth of data.

Documentary analysis

The data collected during the implementation of the PPIC process was fed into an Evaluation Report which was compiled by the Pre-school Specialist Co-ordinator of the home-based teaching team. This report summarised the impact that the project had upon the participants.

Log notes from the 'Learning Together' workshops

A random sample of notes taken at the workshops gave evidence of the project's strengths and weaknesses from a different perspective and helped to cross-validate the findings.

Child Involvement Scale

The 'involvement' of the individual child whilst engaged in a range of activities formed a significant part of the new PPIC process. Each home teacher agreed collaboratively with each parent the specific signals of involvement for their child. Then both parties worked together to make detailed and systematic observations of the child whilst engaged in a range of activities in the home environment. These observations were carried out once at the beginning and once at the end of the process.

Adult Engagement Scale

The parents were asked to make structured observations of the home teachers working with their child. Again, these observations were carried out at the beginning and at the end of the process.

Parent Partnership Scale

A third party was involved to make observations of the practitioner working with the parent. Again, the aim was to make the observations at the beginning and end of the process to show progression and development.

Each of the three observation scales were introduced at the initial training for the teaching team and then at each of the workshops for the parents. To help introduce the first two scales a training video was used which gave examples of the different levels for Child Involvement and Adult Engagement. Role play was used to introduce the Parent Partnership Scale which again gave examples of the different levels within the scale and also helped to give some standardisation.

Ethical issues

Ethical issues played a highly significant part in this study. As much of the data were collected in the homes of the children and parents, it was vital that the rights of the parent, children and teachers were valued and respected at all times, to ensure that the study was not intrusive or invasive in any way. All information was sensitively guarded and action was taken so that all the individuals were unidentifiable.

Miles and Huberman (1996), warn us that the inequity of benefits serve to 'jeopardise access and thin out data'. Reciprocity was therefore important to ensure that each teacher and family would benefit from the training and their involvement in the process and from allowing us into their lives.

Reliability and validity

It was important to acknowledge that, for about a third of the time the process was underway, the home teaching team knew that the structures of their service, working conditions and their individual jobs were going to change. These imminent changes had some impact upon the process, particularly at the points where the teachers needed to spend time analysing the data they had collected and when they were reflecting on the whole process.

The teachers and parents also voiced some concerns about the validity and reliability of the data derived from the Adult Engagement Scale. Clearly, the parents understood and agreed with the concept behind making the observation, but found it difficult to make an objective observation because they did not want to 'upset' the teacher or 'jeopardise the relationship'. Nevertheless, the observations did help to inform the discussions which took place during the workshops. Parents found a common language with which to focus on and discuss their child's learning with the teacher and other professionals.

Evaluative evidence

Parents and teachers presented rich and varied accounts of their experiences of the PPIC model as a new development and improvement strategy. Each questionnaire and interview schedule was logged, transcribed and analyzed for use by the Worcester Research Team.

Impact upon the parents

Generally, most of the parents felt that the process had a beneficial impact. Some of the parents felt that the EEL project had enabled them to make more structured and detailed observations of their child which they found to be informative and enlightening. Several parents went on to suggest that being involved with the EEL Project heightened their understanding of their child's needs. As a result, they felt that it had enhanced and developed their own ability to support and extend their child's learning. As one parent said: 'It has made me more aware of (child's) needs. How little he interacts with people. Using the material enabled us to look further into my (child's) actions'. (Log 10: 6)

Most of the parents said they had found the project to be particularly supportive and worthwhile and that it helped them 'to feel less isolated'. Parents found the workshops to be 'worthwhile' because it enabled them to get 'together, to listen and support each other.' One parent felt that it specifically taught her to 'sit back and watch . . . before intervening.' Most of the parents felt that by the end of the EEL process, their own role had evolved and they had formed more of a 'partnership' with the teacher. Some of the parents said that the process helped to generate a 'common language' with the teacher, which in turn helped to promote and enrich the channels of communication between the parent and the teacher.

Impact upon the teachers

All of the teachers were in agreement that the Learning Together workshops were valuable in developing a working relationship with the parent to the benefit of the child. Specifically, the workshops provided an opportunity for parents and teachers to learn together and to focus upon the individual child's needs. As one teacher said: 'Teachers and parents were genuinely coming together as equals to learn about something new. I felt this helped the parents feel more confident and helped the paired relationships within the group and the dynamics of the group as a whole'. (Log 16: 3)

Although most of the teachers responded very positively about the specific observation schedules, in that they were 'useful' and 'produced some significant results', two main concerns were outlined. First, in relation to the Adult Engagement Scale, the teachers were aware that the parents felt apprehensive about making an observation of the teacher with the child. However, they were in agreement with the philosophy behind the observation. Second, the majority of the teachers expressed that by the end of the process, they felt they had not fully analysed the data which they had collected. This issue is one which has generated much discourse among the Research Team. It has brought about a review of the training programme and materials to emphasise the importance of using the data when evaluating practice.

To summarise, the teachers said that the PPIC process had improved their observational skills, enabled the parents and the teachers to reflect upon their current practice and had given the two parties a common language. This in turn helped to empower the parents and consolidate an effective working relationship. Important issues were raised about the observational schedules which will have an impact upon how the PPIC process develops further.

Emerging issues

Three main issues emerged from the major findings of this study. The experiences of the teachers and the parents became apparent and were found to be inter-related with and supported by theoretical perspectives.

First, it became apparent that parents positively enjoyed and found benefits in their role as strategic partners in the research. After training, the PPIC model facilitated parents to investigate, enquire, discover, plan, monitor, and evaluate and also gave them access to easily assimilated research techniques. Carpenter (1997) claims that there has been very little or even no evidence of parents actu-ally being involved in this way and being 'allowed to take the reins of research'. He advocates a new, exciting and innovative approach to research, that of the 'parent as researcher' paradigm. He transposes the role of researcher upon the parents because they are considered to be the 'natural enquirer within the family – the seeker of knowledge and information that will illuminate needs within their family and specifically in relation to the child with a disability'. Carpenter (1997) goes on to emphasise that 'if we truly wish to empower parents of children with disabilities, then part of that enabling process must be to offer them, as an option, the role of researcher' and so embrace 'parent inclusive patterns of research' (Carpenter 1997: 171).

Second, parents and teachers found that opportunities for collaborative learning were highly valuable. The fact that both parents and teachers were 'learning together' helped to broaden channels of communication, developed a sense of collaboration and enhanced professional partnerships in a non threat-ening and positive way. It encouraged professionals and parents to come together, to engage in dialogue, to share their experiences and struggles. This concept appears to be analogous to what Dahlberg and Asen (1994) refer to as an 'associative' model which above all encompasses civic participation and democracy. Dahlberg and Asen (1994: 166) promote arenas or forums which encourage 'lively dialogue' within which 'early childhood education and care are placed within a larger societal context and where questions concerning children's positions are made vivid'. Through the 'learning together' workshops it was apparent that both the parents and the teachers were able to share information about the child and begin to develop a 'common language' which helped to instil and consolidate more active day-to-day dialogue. This dialogue was based upon the informal conversations, everyday examples, observations and evocative images of the individual child's development.

Third, the parents expressed that the 'learning together' forums were beneficial because they enabled them to get together in a supportive and accepting environ-ment. Authors from various disciplines (Kelly 1963; Erikson 1982; Rogers 1983; Maslow 1987; Hornby 1995; Csikzentmihalyi 1997) help us to conceptualise this notion and explain the importance of encouraging parents to discuss and work through their emotions, to begin to redevelop personal constructs, realise social adaptation and to actualise their own sense of self and well-being to became more effective parents. Margy Whalley, Head of Pen Green Centre for Under Fives, has pioneered a community development approach and has successfully worked with parents to involve them in their child's education. The Centre has developed a radically different approach from that of conventional adult education to provide a community based approach focused upon group support. Whalley (1994) clearly identifies with the work of Freire (1972), an outstanding figure on libertarian education. He believed people should come together to engage in critical dialogue to develop individual confidences and hopes. He disregards the traditional authoritarian teacher–learner model and promotes interactive group work based upon shared investigations, 'characterised by a complex of ideas, concepts, hopes, doubts, values and challenges in dialectical interaction with their opposites, striving towards fulfilment' (Freire 1972: 106).

The new PPIC process is in its early developmental stages, but essentially it aims not only to evaluate and improve pre-school provision for young children with special educational needs, but also to exemplify a new approach, that of the 'parent as researcher paradigm' (Carpenter 1997). Clearly, the evidence gathered so far indicates that there are benefits to be reaped from collaborative learning which includes parents and teachers learning together in a supportive and empowering domain, respecting each others' roles and the unique information parents hold about their child.

APPENDIX: PARENT PARTNERSHIP SCALE

PARTNERSHIP QUALITIES POINT 5	Totally facilitates partnership POINT 5	Mainly facilitates partnership but has evidence of some non-partnership qualities POINT 4	Neither partnership or non-partnership qualities predominate POINT 3	Mainly non-partnership qualities but has evidence of some partnership qualities POINT 2	Total non-partnership POINT 1	NON-PARTNERSHIP QUALITIES POINT 1
SENSITIVITY Adult: (i) uses minimal encouragement (ii) looks at the speaker most of the time – adjusts the degree of looking to the context (iii) uses open questions (iv) uses clarifying questions (v) demonstrates empathy (vi) has a positive warm tone						**SENSITIVITY** Adult: (i) shows distractible behaviour (ii) does not maintain eye-contact (iii) uses 'closed' questions (iv) does not use questions which tentatively clarify parents' viewpoint (v) does not demonstrate empathy by accurate listening (vi) has a distant, negative tone
STIMULATION Interaction: (i) worker summarises parents' model (ii) worker raises contradictions (iii) worker identifies themes (iv) worker tentatively suggests alternative interpretations (v) worker gives information in jargon free language (vi) worker invites two way negotiation (vii) worker shares knowledge						**STIMULATION** Interaction: (i) presses own interpretation of adult's model in a dogmatic manner (ii) is unaware of evidence of contradictions (iii) fails to recognise connecting themes (iv) dictates meaning (v) uses jargon (vi) prevents the adult from engaging in meaningful discussion (vii) does not offer information
EMPOWERMENT Adult: (i) helps to clarify options (ii) helps to evaluate options (iii) supports the development of action plans (iv) encourages ongoing evaluation of the process (v) encourages families to make final decision in all areas						**EMPOWERMENT** Adult: (i) does not clarify options (ii) does not help to evaluate and choose between options (iii) does not facilitate clear planning (iv) does not encourage adult to review and evaluate the process (v) dictates final decision

References

Quotations on page 66 are taken from the unpublished log kept by the Worcester Research Team where the reactions of parents and teachers to the PPIC model are transcribed.

Bertram, A. (1996) *Effective Early Childhood Educators: Developing a Methodology for Improvement*, unpublished PhD thesis, Coventry University.

Carpenter, B. (1997) *Families in Context*, London: David Fulton Publishing.

Csikszentmihalyi, M. (1997) *Living Well – The Psychology of Everyday Life*, London: Weidenfeld & Nicholson.

Dahlberg, G. and Asen, G. (1994) *Evaluation and Regulation: A Question of Empowerment*, in P. Moss, and A. Pence, *Valuing Quality in Early Childhood*, London: Paul Chapman Publishing.

Erikson, E. (1982) *The Life Cycle Completed*, London: Norton Publishing.

Freire, P. (1972) *Pedagogy of the Oppressed*, London: Macmillan.

Hornby, G. (1995) *Working with Parents of Young Children with Special Needs*, London: Cassell.

Kelly, G. (1963) *A Theory of Personality: the Psychology of Personal Constructs*, London: Norton Publishing.

Lincoln, Y. and Guba, G. (1985) *Naturalistic Inquiry*, London: Sage Publishing.

Laevers, F. (1994) *The Innovative Project 'Experiential Education and the Definition of Quality in Education*, Belgium: Leuven University Press.

Maslow, A. (1987) *Motivation and Personality*, London: Harper & Row.

Miles, M. and Huberman, M. (1996) *Qualitative Data Analysis*, London: Sage Publishing.

Pascal, et al. (1996) *Evaluating and Developing Quality in Early Childhood Settings: A Professional Development Programme*, Worcester: Amber Publishing Company.

Pascal, C. and Bertram, A. (1997) *Effective Early Learning. Case Studies in Improvement*, London: Hodder & Stoughton.

Robson, C. (1995) *Real World Research*, London: Blackwell.

Rogers, C. (1983) *Freedom to Learn*, London: Charles Merrill Publishing.

Whalley, M. (1994) *Learning to be Strong*, London: Hodder & Stoughton.

Yin, R. (1989) *Case Study Research*, London: Blackwell Publishing.

Chapter 7

Play Partners

Parental involvement in a pre-school project for children with communication difficulties

Fleur Griffiths

This chapter describes parental involvement in a multi-professional intervention for pre-school children with communication difficulties. Parent support group sessions aim to empower parents to become responsive play partners with their children. Parents gain insight through the use of parable rather than precept, and create their own solutions instead of simply following expert professional advice. Instead of learning from direct instruction, both parents and children take turns and converse around joint activities. Conversational exchange in natural contexts is believed to be at the heart of speaking and understanding. To be avoided are strategies that teach elements of language in a structured manner with a high level of adult control. Such unequal relationships are seen to militate against play partnerships. Children with communication difficulties are believed to need more not less exposure to such facilitative play partners.

The intervention model

Four of us met together for the first time in September 1997. We were the inter-professional team of teacher, support teacher, speech and language therapist and educational psychologist. We were faced with a common challenge for practitioners: to translate a successful 'bid' for funds into an educational reality. We knew the 'model' outlined by the local Health Trust and Education Authority to the charity I CAN, which funds and evaluates new intervention for children with speech and language difficulties nation-wide. The 'model' of intervention was characterised by its commitment to:

- Inclusive education
- Inservice support to nurseries
- Parental involvement

We understood that pre-school children, judged to have 'specific' language difficulties would be selected by the community speech and language therapy service. Our initiative would reach these children, their parents and their nurseries. Because the community speech and language therapy service has found that summertime 'blocks' of input have proved effective, it was proposed that we give intensive 'nursery' intervention for a spell of four weeks, outreaching homes and nurseries before and after the I CAN experience. The extra help would be additional to the children's regular nursery placement , so there would be no uprooting of children from their neighbourhood settings. Our I CAN nursery would move from area to area, once again to ensure a local base and to allow easy access to parents. Parents would be involved as partners in the scheme and have daily access to staff to share concerns. They would be invited to attend a weekly support group, while the children were in session. This was the rhetoric and it was up to us to make it happen.

One school year later, we were able to give a joint presentation of our way of working to our I CAN sponsors and colleagues. This was largely a descriptive account of what we do on a daily, practical basis and although we were in harmony about our methods, we had never articulated any theory underpinning our joint practice. Afterwards, we discussed what was driving our practice and expressed our common beliefs.

Our rationale

We were in agreement about the kind of environment and type of interactions with children, which we favoured to promote language development. We all believed that both assessment and interventions were best achieved in natural-istic play settings and that conversational exchange was at the heart of learning to talk and understand. We all felt uncomfortable with a research paradigm that sought to evaluate the success of the intervention by comparing pre and post estimates of language skill, as measured in normative tests. Instead, we looked for improvements in listening and attention, and in the confidence to initiate conversations. We were uneasy with a medical model which grouped children in sets with the same 'diagnosis' i.e. semantic disorders separate from phonological ones, so that the efficacy of the 'medicine' of intervention could be judged. Mixed groups allowed complementary skills to be used and made for better conversa-tional partners. Being able to take turns in a conversation around a joint activity was our chief aim.

We were aware of the turn-taking nature of early communication (Camainoni and Nadel 1993;Trevarthen 1979), and that the first exchanges between mothers and infants had the to and fro pattern of a prototype conversation. The research on games' formats by Carolyn Smith (1995), working as an educational psy-chologist with children with autistic spectrum disorders in the Isle of Wight, accorded with our contention that it is necessary to establish earlier processes of inter-personal non-verbal exchange, before attempting to promote later stages of expressive language. We agreed with her that games give the chance for joint attention around an action. The players in the game then share the same meanings and memories (Bruner 1983). Further games (see Mackay and Watson 1989) can centre on common events in the children's lives, like shopping or cooking. Research (Nelson 1985) has shown that young children can cope with representing such well-known events, keeping to the correct temporal sequence in the telling. We furthermore believed that meaningful interactions should continue to guide conversation (Webster 1987), and that children and parents are the unacknowledged 'experts' from whom professionals can learn about normal conversational interactions. Parents are less likely than teachers to put the child in the ' position of passive recipient of a prescribed range of language concepts, which are taught separate from the natural contexts in which they might occur' (Webster 1987 :27).

Even the most well-meaning attempts of teachers to join in children's play can silence and alienate children, when the adult is more concerned to make teaching capital than to share an important experience; more keen to question about concepts of space, time, distance or money than to 'keep the flow of speech going by entering in to the spirit of the play' (Wood and Attfield 1996:98). We knew that the best 'ecology of language learning' (Wells 1981) was created when:

> The responsive partner listens to what the child has to say, hands conversation back to the child and allows time to reply. A topic of conversation is sustained by relating each utterance to the child's previous turn and to the context. However limited the child's contribution, a good partner may expand, clarify and paraphrase the child's intended meaning. Empathic responses or social oil, encourage the child to say more, as do personal contributions. Avoided are high control responses such as drilling, open questions or display questions, correcting, enforced repetition or imitation. The rule of thumb is 'only connect', concentrate on sharing understanding with the child.
>
> (Webster 1987 :27)

The term 'conversational disability' (McTear 1985) has been used to describe children with semantic/pragmatic problems, and since children with phonological impairments can shy away from communication, all the children in our groups could be said to need help to converse successfully. Our feeling was that special children need *more* not less exposure to responsive partners. The reason for their failure could be that they have had curtailed experience of interactions in their earliest years. Once they get to nursery, it may be that they do not come on spontaneously because they retreat into safe activities and routines and avoid notice, rather than risk incomprehension and frustration. Parental observations of their children before and after our intervention will be quoted later in support of this feeling.

It would seem logical (or a matter of integrity) to approach parents in a similar way to their children: to listen, respond, expand and connect with their concerns and hopes. As with the children, we wished to avoid direct instruction believing the parents could learn to meet their own children's needs more effectively through 'a mixture of encouragement and observation of other people and by being made to feel valued and welcome in the group' (Campion 1992 :142). When asked what they would most like to see happening as a priority, invariably the overwhelming hope was to be able to 'have a proper conversation' with their children. Since the needs of the children were so diverse and therefore the experience of the carers so varied, wanting to converse represented common ground. Our emphasis on conversation with the children was, therefore, mirrored in our parental groups. A similar emphasis is to be found in the Hanen Programme (Manolson 1992;Watson 1995). Like the Hanen programme, we were using video clips of interactions with the children as illustrations of good practice. Many parents liked to see their children close-up in this way, without risking the disruption that their direct presence in the classroom might cause.

Support group sessions

Welcomes and name games

Parents were invited to get into the shoes of the children and think what it might be like to be landed in a new group, even of just eight people. We would do some of the things we were expecting from the children. You need to know names to approach strangers, and so we played name games and greeting games. To play the games, we expect the children to sit in a circle and wait their turn e.g. to pass the ball to someone by name. We want them to *listen* to each other and *talk in turn*, perhaps with a special object to pass around to denote the speaker. We introduce them to the 'round' (see Brandes and Phillips 1990) and this was to be our mechanism for ensuring that everyone, children and parents alike, could have a voice and choose to 'pass' at will. The parents play the same kind of games, not just as ice-breakers but as an exercise of empathy with their children. Parents who would have felt embarrassed playing games or doing role-plays, had a go because they were persuaded that the activities made sense in the context of understanding their children better.

Listening and attention

The children are alerted to 'good listening' and 'good looking', by picture and demonstration. These are the prerequisite to any successful interaction. So, as adults, we practised listening in pairs on the Co-counselling model so that we could reflect on the factors that helped and hindered communication. We listened to each other talking about our children, the facts and the feelings. We kept confidence and reported back only the information agreed.

A round of news about what our children CAN do

Our conversations about our children, sometimes even within their hearing, can centre on worries and deficits. We were going to think about *conversations for big ears*, and deliberately air good news when they were listening in! The importance of self-esteem and confidence came up here.

A round of 'what I would like to see happening as a result of coming here'

This allowed for discussion of realistic hopes, and an assertion of the power of parents to change things, rather than rely on the 'experts'.

Further topics

Being a play partner

Using and abusing questioning

A round of 'Questions that I would like to ask'

Learning from making mistakes

Correcting and protecting

A round of 'How my child is like and not like other children'

Can't and Won't

Attention seeking behaviours (see Mellor 1997)

A round of 'Changes I have seen in my child and myself'

Because the 'how' is more important than the 'what', the content of the sessions is deliberately confined to a list of possible topics which provide the backdrop to the sessions. What happens depends very much on what parents contribute. A degree of improvisation is therefore necessary. Parents often sought direct advice, which was not forthcoming. Our method was to use parable rather than precept, allegory rather than advice to promote insight. Ready for use were a fund of apt stories, many of which were gleaned from a social work colleague, Eric Harvey, who used stories to illuminate the child's point of view (reproduced in Beaver 1996: 199ff).

The following story illustrates our method. The story (which is a real instance in this case) was prompted by a father asking directly what he should do to get his son, Simon, to do something else besides pull a train round and round. His wish for the future was to have 'a proper conversation with the lad'. The reply to his question was left for him to fathom out from the story, and no teaching points needed to be elicited. The story went as follows:

> Once upon a time, I visited a nursery to see Jim. He was reported to have done nothing for months except drag a train in circles, watching the wheels turn. He had resisted strongly all attempts to move him on to other choices

on offer, refusing even to engage in eye contact. I approached and lay alongside him on the floor to share his view. Slowly, I lined up some play people to be passengers and stood them on a station alongside the route. As the train came past I called out that people wanted to get on the train. Jim became aware of me, and glanced at the station. The second time around, the train came to a halt and I was allowed to put on a passenger. Gradually, Jim came to expect passengers to get on and off at more than one station. He began to call out 'Get on!' and 'Station'. Next, I put a cow on the track, which does happen in one of the Tank Engine books. Jim smiled as he put the cow out of the way. This game was repeated for the rest of the play time, and then uncharacteristically, Jim grabbed a piece of chalk and drew a circular 'track'. I followed him and chased his lines right behind him. He ran on fast wanting me to keep up as in a game of chase. His teacher was amazed to see him laughing and having fun.

Later on at home, Jim greeted me with a smile and tugged me to the sofa to sit down and repeat the chasing game with pencils and paper. His mother was surprised how still he sat and for how long he concentrated on sharing an activity with me. With this experience as a starting point, Jim started to join in with his mum as a play partner.

By the end of the I CAN intervention, this father talked of the changes he had seen:

> I have changed my way of being with Simon. Since he was two, I have tried to do as I was advised. . . . Our sessions got worse and worse, because I was acting like a *dictator*, and Simon shut me out and kept his mouth shut. Now I am *a mate*, and we play together and he talks to me. We have little conversations. He will now do all sorts of different things, like drawing and painting which he would not touch before and he likes me to join in.

After this in the group, the shorthand for being a responsive play partner was 'the train way'. Another shorthand was playing 'knocky nine doors'. To illuminate the child's perspective, attention-seeking behaviour was discussed by analogy with the game of knocking on doors and running away to a safe distance to enjoy the irate and exasperated response. If you knock on a door and no one ever comes, you leave this house out and stick to the one where there is most reaction, however cross and threatening. Children quickly learn how to play knocky-nine-doors on us!

Parents are free to apply the story as they will. Such stories make for laughter and relaxation, and in such a mood, parents do not feel so defensive or to blame. They feel themselves to be in good company.

Sometimes, we play the same games as the children to increase our repertoire and to learn along with them. One session, we watched a video clip of the children playing a parachute game. Each child held a loop on the outer circle of the parachute, and at a signal from the teacher, made it swell up enough to allow each child in turn to cross underneath it. They travelled in different ways: crawling, jumping, marching, dancing or moving fast or slow; with big steps or little steps. They listened out for their names and for single-word instructions and collaborated together to make the game happen. We could, then, have considered what the children were learning from this game, but before this we handled the parachute ourselves. Comments afterwards from parents were the more insightful. One grandfather said:

> I thought at first that they were just having fun, but I see that they were learning about language like 'under' and 'over'; 'up' and 'down'; 'fast' and 'slow'; 'big' and 'little'. They were also doing what the teacher said and listening. Playing was not just doing whatever you felt like without any discipline.

This spokesman for the playway to learning was a convert. Getting the message across about the value of play with facilitative partners, and the need for challenge could not have been more ably expressed.

Often in their anxiety to catch their failing children up to standard, parents curtail play activity and plug pre-school readiness with drills about colours, numbers, and letters, with a barrage of educational toys. Such activities, all too often, end in fraught lessons with listless or hostile learners.

Feedback from parents

Parents were asked to comment on any changes in their children and in themselves, and they made the following comments:

> ANDREW has changed so much. He now talks all the time when he used to clam up. His confidence has risen – he believes he will be understood. At nursery, he was on the edge of the circle; now, he has many friends. He is choosing a wider variety of activities, instead of opting for sand all the time. Nursery staff have noted that he is not so shy and will join in.
>
> He would like to come to I CAN even on a Sunday! He will even tackle speech games at home if they are the I CAN ones and we follow the pattern set. He is more likely to practise speech sounds, instead of avoiding.
>
> I, myself, have more understanding of what is naughty and stubborn. I can stop and think, 'Why is he doing this?'

> BEN has improved a lot – listening and talking. He is aware of people now – he has learned all their names. He is not shut off – he wants to join in; he wants to be there. He is now asking, 'What's this?', and nudging me to answer. He used to be hyper-active but he is much calmer. He joins in with me now – he used to do his own thing and ignore me.
>
> For me, to be in the group has made me feel I am not on my own.

CLARA's confidence has gone forward. Visiting relatives, they could not believe the change. Before, she would not participate or get involved. Now, she joins in and can carry on small conversations.

DAVID has found his voice. In the car, he used to be silent, but now he sings out. He is giving a vocal response instead of silence. He is choosing more things at Nursery – he used to go to the same place every day. He has more confidence – to have a go. He has the will to pipe up! Nursery has noticed this too. He used to go in a temper and head bang, but now, he can give a mouthful!
It was good to see the therapy in action and be part of it.

EMILY has calmed down and is more confident. We can work together – before, she did not want to know. I am talking slower and she is copying off me. I am getting her to look at me and to take notice. I am talking to her about what we do – while washing up for instance. She is talking now because she really wants to. I now know better the things she understands and the things she does not understand.

FRED's confidence has grown. He used to play by himself – he now joins in the home corner with others. He wants people to 'come and look' what he has done. He understands taking 'turns'.

Labelling

The children above represent the range of language impairment. Those children considered to be on the autistic continuum have been included and also those queried as having semantic/pragmatic disorders. It could be thought that children who find symbolic play incomprehensible would be untouched by our naturalistic approach. In fact, it has been such children who appear to have made the most noticeable gains.
Diagnosing and labelling such young children, apart from being hard to do with assurance, is of dubious merit. No longer is there anything to be gained by taking sides in the nature/nurture debate, and the interactive position is generally taken. We know that children are both moulded by their life experiences and able to modify their environments. Even so, it was interesting to find cases which pointed to a predominantly environmental, rather than genetic aetiology. For example, Michelle was described by her nursery carers as 'odd', in that she avoided eye contact and imaginative play with others. She favoured solitary, scholarly activities involving letters and numbers. She was upset by any interruptions, and distressed by strangers and changes in routine. At I CAN, she avoided the house corner and was visibly upset when it changed to a Macdonald's during a play sequence. Unlike the others, she did not enjoy the pretence of licking a playdoh lolly, anxiously calling out 'NO! no! it's only playdoh!'.

It transpired that Michelle's mother was depressed, worn down by the active demands of two small children. She was worried about their health and safety. She was bored by being at home all day without any adult conversation. She, in spite of her shyness, attended all the parent sessions, enjoying the break. In one session, she commented that Michelle was playing shops, but froze on seeing her as if she were doing something wrong. Michelle's mother took the new step of joining in the make-believe, and after the initial awkwardness, the pair relaxed into the fun of it. Michelle continued to be a serious and rather literal-minded child, but became the leader in the nursery for lotto-type games. Games with rules and clear turn-taking, provided her with the necessary inroad to social interaction, and the 'semantic/pragmatic' label was peeling away.

Other examples of children with little exposure to play partners have emerged, and they have forged ahead given the help. Those more mildly autistic children have benefited from play situations engineered by sensitive adults, incorporating the scripts and social formulas they have heard. This is more than parroting because the scripts copied appear in proper contexts and are socially mediated. Once the children say the expected thing in a given situation, they are more likely to become part of the group dynamic. They are being helped through the phases of being an actor /agent in shared play sequences, and become initiators and negotiators of play events. The role of the mediating adult: scaffolding the learning; oiling the flow of conversation; putting in timely repairs and re-runs, is of vital importance. Voicing disagreement with someone's favourite colour /food/ programme is often a more powerful goad to speaking out than too much assenting protection. Particularly striking, are the strategies used to promote laughter and relaxation: for example there is the pantomime formula of 'Oh, no, you won't! – Oh, yes I will!' or the playfully provocative 'You'll never guess' or 'I bet you can't . . .'

However strongly we favour situations relevant to the child's interests, we are not naïve enough to think that children will pick up language naturally without facilitative play partners. We take on board the warning:

> Conversation is such a common human activity that we are in danger of taking it for granted or of under-estimating the complex 'work' that is involved in engaging successfully in a conversation. In fact, the belief that conversation is natural is a major barrier to serious research into children's conversational development and, as a consequence, into the nature of conversational disability.
>
> (McTear 1993 :1)

References

Beaver, R. (1996) *Educational Psychology Casework*, London: Jessica Kingsley.

Brandes, D. and Phillips, H. (1990) *Gamesters' Handbook*, Cheltenham: Stanley Thornes.

Bruner, J. (1983) *Child Talk: Learning to Use Language*, Oxford: Oxford University Press.

Camainoni, L. and Nadel, J. (1993) *New Perspectives in Early Communicative Development*, London: Routledge.

Campion, J. (1992) *Working with Vulnerable Children: Early Intervention*, London: Cassell.

Mackay, M and Watson, J. (1989) 'Games for Promoting Communication', *British Journal of Special Education* 16: 58–61.

McTear, M. (1985) *Children's Conversation*, Oxford: Blackwell.

McTear, M. (1993) *Assessing Children's Conversational skills*, Conference Paper, Department of Speech, University of Newcastle on Tyne.

Manolson, A.(1992) *It takes Two to Talk: A Parents' Guide to Helping Children Communicate*, Toronto: Hanen Centre Publications.

Mellor, N. (1997) *Attention-Seeking*, Bristol: Lucky Duck.

Nelson, K. (1985) *Event Representation and Cognitive Development*, Chicago IL: Lawrence Erlbaum.

Smith, C. (1995) *A Developmental Approach to Pre-linguistic Intervention*, Paper for Educational Psychologists' Interest Group (Gateshead Teachers' Centre) in preparation for a doctoral thesis from the University of Portsmouth.

Trevarthen, C. (1979) 'Communication and Co-operation in Early Infancy: a Description of Primary Inter-subjectivity', in M. Bullowa (ed.) *Before Speech: the Beginnings of Human Communication*, Cambridge: Cambridge University Press.

Watson, C. (1995) *Making Hanen Happen*, Toronto: Hanen Centre Publications.

Webster, A. (1987) 'Enabling Language Acquisition: the developmental evidence', *British Psychological Society: Division of Educational and Child Psychology Newsletter* 27: 25–31.

Wells, G. (1981) *Learning Through Interaction: the Study of Language Development*, Cambridge: Cambridge University Press.

Wood, E. and Attfield, J. (1996) *Play, Learning and the Early Childhood Curriculum*, London: Paul Chapman.

For further information on I CAN's Early Years Series for children with speech and language impairment contact:

I CAN
4 Dyer's Buildings
Holborn
London ECIN 2QP
Tel: 0870 010 4066
Fax: 0870 010 4067

Chapter 8

What is normal?

Helen Penn

A *baby is a European*

A baby is a European
He does not eat our food
He drinks from his own water pot

A baby is a European
He does not speak our tongue
He is cross when his mother understands him not

A baby is a European
He cares very little for others
He forces his will upon his parents

A baby is a European
He is always sensitive
The slightest scratch on his skin results in an ulcer
(Chinweizu 1988: 413)

The changing status of disability

This chapter reviews a range of ideas about normality and disability and considers their implications for practice in working with young children.

What is normal? I have been rereading some of the books by the novelist Iris Murdoch. The plot of *The Bell*, one of the earlier novels, written in the 1950s, hinges entirely on the homosexuality of the principal character Michael, and how his life is destroyed, not once, but twice, by revelations of his homosexual yearnings, which he tried desperately to suppress. By the 1990s Iris Murdoch portrays homosexuality quite differently. In *The Green Knight* it is a normal and unremarkable phenomenon. What was once regarded as a perversion and matter of shame, is now described as a pleasurable commonplace. There are many such examples of major changes in attitude and these changes are going on before our eyes. Already in the USA in one state and in twenty-five major cities, white Americans are a minority – Hispanics and blacks represent the majority, if not the dominant culture, and by 2080 it is predicted that white Americans will be a minority in the USA as a whole. How will this affect the study – indeed an industry in America – of child development which will no longer be able to take white middle-class expectations as a norm for behaviour, or English as its first language ?

These changes matter because they suggest that definitions of 'special needs' are not constant but differ from time to time and place to place, and the toleration of those defined as having special needs, and the treatment offered to them also differs. Even where there is a recognizable, genetically caused disability such as Down's Syndrome, attitudes towards children who carry the gene have changed considerably. As late as the 1960s they were regarded as largely ineducable, and were often hospitalized. Now many are allowed to take part in mainstream schooling. Corker and French (1999) make the distinction between 'impairment' which they see as a physical attribute of the body, and 'disability' which they argue is socially created. In their book *Disability Discourse* they present a series of narratives from men and women with impairments to illustrate how different from each other those impairments and their treatments are, and how 'disability' has become a blanket description which obscures very different realities for individuals. The language itself used to describe 'special needs' or 'disability' needs continual modification.

Categories of disability

The largest category of those with special needs today are children who are labelled as having emotional and behavioural disorders. Such children also come disproportionately from poor homes and from ethnic minority backgrounds, so much so, that they may be targeted for 'early intervention' even before they demonstrate any disorder, on the grounds that prevention is better than cure. But as Iglesias and Quinn (1997) suggest, to describe any group of people as inadequate parents at risk of producing poorly behaved children on the grounds of low income or ethnic origin, begs many questions about dominant societal attitudes and values. Priscilla Alderson and Chris Goody (1998) in their book *Enabling Education* argue on the basis of their research in 'special' and 'normal' schools that conventionally accepted contemporary categories of behaviour such as Learning Difficulty, ASD (Autistic Spectrum Disorder) and EBD (Emotional and Behaviour Disorder) do not stand up to close scrutiny, and there is confusion about assessment, treatment, and evaluation of the effects of treatment.

McDermott (1993) goes still further and argues that schooling – or the kind of schooling on offer currently – creates disability rather than addresses it. In an article entitled 'The acquisition of a child by a learning disability', he claims that the schooling system is inherently competitive and that failure is the other side of the coin to success; the inevitability of failure is built into the system, and success, by definition, entails comparison with others who have failed. Yet failure is viewed as a personal rather than societal characteristic. Psychologists and psychiatrists, who use the apparently neutral technological language of assessment and treatment thereby give credibility to a discriminatory situation.

> By the normal line of reasoning, the child is the unit of analysis and the (learning) disability is a mishap that scars a child's road to competence. . . . Although the folk theory has it that the traits – an inability to pay attention, an occasional lapse in word access, trouble with phonics etc. – belong to the child and are the source of both the disordered behaviour and the subsequent label, it is possible to argue that it is the labels that precede any child's entry into the world and that these labels, well-established resting places in adult conversation, stand poised to take their share from each new generation . . . in allowing schools to become the site of sorting for recruitment into the wider social structure, we may have gone too far for the collective good. We may have made it necessary to invent occasions – millions of them – to make learning disabilities institutionally and unnecessarily consequential.
>
> (McDermott 1993: 273)

Rose (1987) also argues that psychology is about establishing normative data and defining what is pathological; and using historical evidence, he attempts to show how the history of psychology can be described as a series of attempts to diagnose, conceptualize and regulate pathologies of conduct according to the social mores of the time.

Another theoretical challenge to the categorization of disability is from the new field of the sociology of childhood. This body of research examines children as a social group, who experience the oppression of other, more powerful, social groups, and gives particular emphasis to the direct and unmediated views of children themselves (James and Prout 1990). The views of vulnerable or disabled children about their assessment, labelling and treatment are beginning to be explored and may well lead to new insights and approaches in the field of disability (Goody and Alderson 1998).

Culture, society and disability

The same traits or dispositions which may mark a child as normal and ordinary in some situations, in others appear exceptional and offensive to common decency. The poem which opens this chapter, by a poet from Togo, neatly illustrates the point that childhood and normality are socially constructed. The 'self-confident loquaciousness', a child bursting with self-esteem and richly articulate, which is an ideal of American childhood (Levine *et al.* 1994) would simply be regarded as an embarrassment in many Majority (third) world societies; conversely the helpfulness, docility and obedience expected of children in some societies, would be regarded as repression, over-control and exploitation by many Minority (first) world child experts. Child development, as a discipline, as Woodhead (1998) has pointed out, is far from universal as a system of explanation; on the contrary it is rooted in Anglo-American concepts of normality and progress.

To consider this argument from another angle, the kinds of assessment, therapeutic and medical support we may consider essential in dealing with disability are particular to our society, rather than universal. A number of writers (Wessels 1996; Richman 1996) have made similar points that minority world ideas about support and therapy cannot simply be exported and for example, children traumatized by war and separation may respond better to indigenous healers than to 'expert' help. Reynolds has carried out several studies of childhood in South Africa and Zimbabwe and in her latest book on traditional healers and childhood in Zimbabwe she examines the successful role of traditional healing in conflict resolution. 'Therapeutic movements (traditional healers) . . . can contribute to the redefinition of reality and can imagine alternatives and the consequences of such alternatives if taken' (Reynolds, 1996: xxv).

Vygotsky, whose theories about socially situated learning have to an extent superseded those of Piaget, was a co-founder of the Institute of Defectology in Russia (see Rieber and Carton 1993). 'Defectology' was the notion that some children are functioning so far below normal expectations, for a variety of reasons, that very special inputs are necessary to try to remedy the situation. 'Defectology', which now sounds an offensive label, was, paradoxically, intended as the opposite, a refusal to write off any child, whatever her circumstances or behaviour; a radical belief that *all* human beings were sufficiently complex and had the internal resources to be educable, and with adequate professional help, to learn to compensate for their disadvantages.

> The world pours, through a large funnel as it were, in thousands of stimuli, drives and callings; . . . the actualized behaviour is but an infinitesimal part of the possible behaviour. Man is full of unrealized opportunities at any given moment . . .
>
> (Rieber and Carton 1993: 14)

This notion that children could be transformed through education was widespread in ex-communist countries. Many children with disabilities were institutionalized, in the hope, often never realized, that intensive treatment would be forthcoming (and as a consequence much of the involvement of aid agencies in transitional countries is now concerned with programmes to de-institutionalize children). However, where this approach has been seen to be effective, it has been taken up in the West. The Peto Institute in Hungary has become well known for its conductive education, that is attempts to rehabilitate physically disabled children through intensive exercise programmes, in order that they can then cope better with everyday life. Feuerstein, an Israeli psychologist, has taken a similar approach to mediated learning for children with learning disabilities. His model, widely used in Israel and the USA, also argues for intensive and highly specialized rehabilitation before children can enter mainstream facilities, and one of his books (1988) has the disturbing title *Don't accept me as I am: Helping Retarded People to Excel*.

Some physical disabilities are easily curable with basic medicine or surgery, others offer no cure; but by far the majority of disabilities and the majority of treatments exist in a limbo of medical and psychological uncertainty; there are different ways of being and behaving, different behaviours and modes of being are more or less acceptable according to time and place. The interpretion and treatment of behaviour and disability is almost always problematic.

Medicine and ethics

Medical advances in genetic engineering, prenatal screening and care of premature babies have given rise to many new ethical considerations about disability. Whilst knowledge about how to detect genetic conditions is advancing rapidly, knowledge about how to treat or cure them is far less certain. As Alderson points out, 'The widening gap between diagnosis and effective treatment is filled mainly by one medical intervention: the option to terminate affected pregnancies' (Alderson 1999). If disability can be predicted in advance, and can be avoided by contraception or termination of pregnancy, if a medical misdiagnosis can lead to huge compensation claims, what are the implications for those who are born disabled? As Alderson comments:

> These choices accentuate the conflicts between parents and their offspring, between present and future generations, between able and disabled people, and people who are seen as dependents and those who support them, whether personally or collectively as taxpayers. . . . Prenatal services which convey explicit or covert messages about parents' rights to a perfect baby can also convey subliminal beliefs about passivity and even helplessness, that parents cannot and should not have to cope with the extra demands which disability can bring . . . a 'perfect child' is assumed to be hard enough and a disabled child could be an impossible burden.
>
> (Alderson 1999)

Genetic screening and other medical interventions change ideas of disability, so that instead of seeing it as a 'natural' aspect of life, that is understanding coping with disability as one effort amongst many that parents make, disability is more likely to be seen as something avoidable and unnecessary. On the other hand, there are other medical developments in relation to the care of premature babies, that are leading to an increase in the number of disabled children, especially severely disabled children. Health planners know that the survival of premature infants is likely to lead to increased health-care costs, not only in the care of neonates, but in the provision of assessment and remedial services at 'child development clinics' and subsequently for the education services in providing for statemented children. Paradoxically, medical intervention assumes that at one stage, everything must be done to prevent disability, yet at a subsequent stage, life must be preserved at all costs. These dilemmas, as medical knowledge and expertise develops, mean that the ethics of intervention will become increasingly important, for parents who have, or who may have a disabled child; for the children themselves experiencing the negative attitudes of others towards their disabilities; and for the wider society which carries a responsibility for support and treatment – and the costs which might ensue.

The role of parents

Involving parents in what was exclusively a medical preserve, that is in the assessment, support and treatment of disability, has been regarded as a radical step. The Portage scheme, in particular, has been praised for offering a convenient and widely usable package, which enables parents and professionals to work together on improving the language, motor and emotional behaviour patterns of young children with disabilities (White 1997). However, many direct interventions with parents in early years assume a family structure in which the mother undertakes the main burden of care, and does not, cannot or should not work. A recent Canadian study of the mothers of disabled children suggests that caring for a disabled child is not necessarily in itself arduous, and may be very pleasurable, but what is wearying is the assumption that because they have a child with a disability, they must therefore expect to be excluded from the workforce (Irwin and Lero 1997). Typically, a child with a disability will be referred to a number of different clinics for various kinds of assessment, monitoring and treatment. I interviewed one group of mothers of disabled children (Penn and Gough 2000) whose children were attending a child development assessment programme. Most of these mothers had been previously working and had hoped to continue after their maternity leave expired.

> There are so many appointments, at least two a week, sometimes four or five. I couldn't possibly work now although I want to. (Machinist)

> I sell books and I work from home and I wouldn't mind taking her with me whilst she's small, but I can't even get an orange badge (for parking) because she is under five, so it's doubly difficult, making deliveries. I need to work. (Book saleswoman)

> I dropped one day a week so I could try to make the appointments and I'm fortunate, her nan helps out. My husband would come to some of the appointments, but he can't get the time off work and there are no weekend or evening appointments. (Midwife)

Previously, institutional care was widely available to the most severely disabled children, although this was painful and often damaging for the children themselves, and parents usually felt highly ambivalent about it. But, for very good reasons, there has been widespread international movement to disband residential care, and in the UK, as in other countries, it is now mostly unavailable. The respite care – or community care – which has replaced it, is of a very short duration. For example, the local authority in which my informants lived offered respite care once a fortnight for a few hours, and very occasionally, for the most severe cases, a night away from home.

Attitudes towards gender equality have also changed considerably. It is now accepted in law that women have as much right to work as men, and that public and/or private support, in the form of childcare, is an acceptable alternative to mothering. Mother–child attachment is no longer seen as the major issue it once was, by psychological researchers or policy makers. Yet this change in attitudes has not yet translated to the mothers of children with disabilities, at least in the UK. Such mothers usually face extra disadvantages if they wish to exercise their entitlements in the labour market, in trying to fit in with the timetables of professionals; in facing a residue of negative attitudes which sees them as abandoning their vulnerable children; and not least, in finding suitable, affordable placements for their children.

The Salamanca Agreement

The UN Declaration on the Rights of the Child has been interpreted by many of those concerned with disability to imply that it is morally wrong to segregate children with disabilities, and they have an entitlement to receive the same educational opportunities as any other children.

The Salamanca Agreement is an international agreement, signed in 1994 by 92 governments and a host of international agencies including UNESCO and UNICEF, which states:

> Every child has a fundamental right to education and must be give the opportunity to achieve and maintain an acceptable level of learning . . . mainstream(regular) education is . . . the most effective means of combatting discriminatory attitudes, creating welcoming communities, building an inclusive society and achieving education for all.
>
> This level should recognize the principle of inclusion and be developed in a comprehensive way by combining pre-school activities and early childhood health care.
>
> (World Needs Conference 1994: Preamble)

Spain, as a major contributor to the Salamanca agreement, has well articulated policies on disability. LOGSE, the Spanish Education Reform Act passed in 1989 includes strong statements on access of children with disabilities to the mainstream. In infant nurseries for example, children with disabilities usually count for two places, and every effort is made to bring the specialist services to the nursery, rather than require parents to attend specialist therapeutic sessions elsewhere (Penn 1997). As suggested above, the fundamental assumption of the

Salamanca agreement, that all children have rights and entitlements whatever their circumstances or condition, is being taken up by major donor agencies, and the integration of children with disabilities in early childhood, as a prototype for later integration, is being developed, for example, by Save the Children, in countries such as China and Laos (Holdsworth 1994).

The position in the UK

A number of recent changes and initiatives in the UK have served to raise the status of early childhood services. But although there may be more services and more money available, the situation noted by Potts has not yet significantly changed.

> The complexity, instability and regional variability of services for pre-school children lead to inequalities in the experiences of young children and their families. Within the current framework, parents may have access to specialist services but they only rarely have the choice of an appropriate service provided in a more comprehensive setting.
>
> (Potts 1992: 5)

Whilst there are some fully integrated settings where children with disabilities can use local facilities and receive specialist support within them, in the UK the most common form of intervention (at least as a first stage) for children who are suspected of 'developmental delay' is at a Child Development Centre. These may be multi-disciplinary, but they are primarily medical in orientation and are usually funded by health authorities. Children are typically given medical and psychological assessments, and monitored through part-time visits, when they may also receive some kind of remedial attention. Depending on the statementing process, the children will then be referred on to what is considered 'the most appropriate' form of provision for them. What is deemed 'most appropriate' will depend on the policy of the local authority towards statementing and integration, and the resources available for additional help such as transport (Kates 1997). Parents may resist these expert assessments, particularly where they involve referral to specialist provision, but as Potts suggests, their choices are often very limited ones, and are unlikely to include any form of childcare. Most childcare is still available in the private, rather than the local authority sector; and because costs are met by the parents directly, this means that the mother of a disabled child may have to pay for additional care and adaptations which may be required, and even then appropriate training and support may not be available to staff.

A further point is that the pressures on mainstream schools to achieve good academic results, and the admission of so many four-year-olds to school, has led to some schools being very intolerant of children who do not fit in. It seems extraordinary that four-year-old children should be excluded from school, but it is not uncommon. The rise in the number of school exclusions is regarded by many commentators as a very worrying trend (Duffield et al. 1995).

Conclusion

As the rest of this book suggests, there are some very positive examples of integration of children with disabilities. This chapter emphasizes that, as a starting point for discussion about practice with young children, it is important to consider the wide range of arguments which have informed the disability debate or will increasingly do so. These include the variety of understandings about disability – and indeed about childhood – which are held in minority and majority world countries; the developments in medical technology; the links between low societal status and disability; and the changing roles of women. Above all, it is important to emphasize the diversity and complexities of children's lives – their lives as they experience them and talk about them, and the lives of those who bring them up. Perhaps the most important, and difficult, message to convey is the need to be both open-minded and well informed when change is happening in front of us.

References

Alderson, P. (1999) 'Prenatal Screening' in I. Carrol and C. Skidmore (eds) *Inventing Heaven. Quakers Confront the Challenges of Genetic Engineering*, Reading: Sowle Press, 42–53.

Alderson P. and Goody, C. (1998) *Enabling Education*, London: Tufnell Press.

Chinweizu (ed.) (1988) *Voices from Twentieth Century Africa: Griots and Towncriers*, London: Faber.

Corker, M. and French, S. (eds) (1999) *Disability Discourse*, Buckingham: Open University Press.

Duffield, J., Riddell, S. and Brown, S.(1995) *Policy, Practice and Provision for Children with Specific Learning Difficulties*, Aldershot: Avebury.

Feuerstein, R., Rand, Y. and Ryndas, J. (1988) *Don't accept me as I am: Helping Retarded People to Excel*, New York: Plenum Press.

Holdsworth, J. (1994) *Lao Integrated Education Programme Report*, London: Save the Children.

Iglesias, A. and Quinn, R. (1997) 'Culture as a Context for Early Intervention' in S. Thurman, J.Cornwell and S. Gottwald (eds) *Contexts of Early Intervention: Systems and Settings*, Baltimore: Paul H. Brookes Publishing, 55–72.

Irwin, S. and Lero, D. (1997) *In Our Way: Childcare Barriers to Full Workforce Participation Experienced by Parents of Children with Special Needs*, Nova Scotia: Breton Books.

James, A. and Prout, A. (eds) (1990) *Constructing and Reconstructing Childhood*, London: Falmer Press.

Kates, D. (1997) 'The Funding Context of Early Intervention' in S. Thurman, J.Cornwell and S. Gottwald (eds) *Contexts of Early Intervention: Systems and Settings*, Baltimore: Paul H. Brookes Publishing, 39–54.

Levine, R., Dixon, S., Levine, S. *et al.* (1994) *Childcare and Culture: Lessons from Africa*, Cambridge: Cambridge University Press.

McDermott, R. (1993) 'The acquisition of a child by a learning disability', in S. Chaiklin and J. Lave (eds) *Understanding Practice: Perspectives on Activity and Context*, Cambridge: Cambridge University Press, 269–305.

Penn, H. (1997) *Comparing Nurseries*, London: Paul Chapman.

Penn, H. and Gough, D. (2000) *Family Support*, forthcoming.

Potts, P. (ed) (1992) *Learning for All: Right from the Start*, Open University Course Reader E242, Unit 5.

Reynolds, P. (1996) *Traditional Healers and Childhood in Zimbabwe*, Ohio: Ohio University Press.

Rieber, R. and Carton, S. (1993) *The Collected Works of L.S. Vygotsky*, vol. 2, *The Fundamentals of Defectology*, New York: Plenum Press.

Richman, N. (1996) *Looking Before and After: Asylum Seekers in the West*, Paper given at SCF conference, *Rethinking the Trauma of War*, London.

Rose, N. (1987) *The Psychological Complex*, London: Routledge.

Wessels, M. (1996) *Assisting Angolan Children Impacted by War: Blending Western and Indigenous Approaches to Healing*, Paper given at UNICEF seminar, Florence.

White, M. (1997) 'A Review of the influences and effects of Portage', in S. Wolfendale (ed) *Working with Parents of SEN Children after the Code of Practice*, London: David Fulton.

Woodhead, M.(1998) '"Quality" in early childhood programmes – a contextually-appropriate approach', *International Journal of Early Years Education*. 6(1).

World Needs Conference on Special Needs Education: Access and Quality (1994) Salamanca: UNESCO/Ministry of Education and Science.

Chapter 9

Behaviour problems in the early years

The conceptualisation of behaviour problems and its relevance to management approaches

Theodora Papatheodorou

Current research has clearly revealed that progressively younger children than ever have been perceived as exhibiting behaviour problems in educational settings. Consequently, management of such problems becomes an important element of the teaching and learning process. Nursery teachers, nursery nurses and all early-years professionals constantly need to use a wide range of management approaches and techniques to handle the wide range of behaviour problems arising in educational settings (Papatheodorou 1995). Indeed, both the Green and White Paper referring to Special Educational Needs have strongly emphasised the need for early identification of and intervention for young children's behavioural difficulties (DfEE 1997; 1998).

Historically, behaviour-management approaches have been influenced by the psychological models dominating the conceptualisation of behaviour problems (Walker and Shea 1988). Various approaches of different theoretical orientation have been developed by professionals working in different disciplines and most of them have been employed in educational settings (Meyhew 1997; Elliot and Place 1998). It is therefore important for the early-years professionals to have a clear understanding of how behaviour problems have been, and still are, conceptualised and what is the relevance of such conceptualisation to the management approaches and techniques developed and used in educational settings (Shea and Bauer 1987; Kerr and Nelson 1989).

In this chapter, the underlying principles of the psychoanalytic, behavioural, cognitive and ecosystemic approaches will be discussed and specific techniques within each approach will be outlined. Such a discussion aims to provide a conceptual framework where teachers and early-years professionals in general can place, or make sense, of their own daily practice in dealing with and managing behaviour in early-years settings.

The psychoanalytic approach

Up to the 1950s and even during the 1960s the medical and psychodynamic models dominated the field of special education. According to these models behaviour problems are seen as the visible symptoms of internal, invisible and unconscious impulses and conflicts (Davie 1986). Both models imply that the problem resides within the individual either in the soma/body (the medical model), or in psyche/soul (psychodynamic theory), or in both psyche and soma (Rhodes 1974). By definition such terms imply that the focus of any approach to manage behaviour problems should be the children themselves.

In the light of these models the psychoeducational approach was developed in order to deal with behaviour problems. Professionals, mainly from the health disciplines, developed and used a range of management techniques such as individual and group psychotherapy, directive and non-directive counselling, family therapy, expressive arts, and 'surface' behaviour management. However, counselling, expressive arts, and 'surface' behaviour management have also been found applicable in educational settings (Shea and Bauer 1987; Walker and Shea 1988). According to the psychoeducational approach, teachers' major goal is to understand why children are behaving as they do and to establish a positive, trusting and meaningful relationship. The psychoeducational approach places emphasis on accepting children as they are, developing a mentally healthy classroom atmosphere, providing order and routine in the classroom schedule, and eliminating external stimuli causing disturbance.

Counselling in particular aims to facilitate children to increase their conscious awareness of distorted perceptions of existing realities, and to provide emotional support in order to reduce their level of frustration (Carpenter and Apter 1988; Davie 1989). It is often used to describe the process of listening to problems, advising on actions and explaining the constraints within which children should operate (Elliot and Place 1998). Counselling is often viewed as something highly skilled, requiring competence and substantial professional training. However, a great deal of counselling is practised by a variety of people who developed their skills through experience, reading, sharing ideas and concerns with others (Murgatroyd 1985). Teachers very often find themselves to be in the latter situation. Although limited, empirical support indicates that counselling in the school context can become highly powerful especially when it is used in parallel with behavioural techniques (Carpenter and Apter 1988; Lavoritano and Segal 1992). Elliot and Place, however, express their concern that counselling may be 'misguidedly used as a euphemism for controlling behaviour' (1998: 11).

On the other hand, expressive arts applied in an appropriate environment and under competent guidance provide children with the opportunity to express their feelings and emotions and to reduce stress and frustration without the danger of conflict with others (Walker and Shea 1988). They are more appropriate for young children, who are generally less capable of verbal communications and less in control of their personal life-style. Expressive arts include free-play, role play and psychodrama, creative movement and dance, music, story-telling, drawing. Most of them have been developed and used by therapists in therapeutic settings by applying specific knowledge and skills. However, most of these activities constitute an important component of any early-years curriculum and part of the life in early-years settings. Therefore early-years professionals can use them to facilitate young children's emotional and affective development by simply applying consistently and sensitively the following rules suggested by Axline (1989):

- to accept children and present themselves as they are, not as they should be;
- to develop a warm and friendly relationship;
- to provide opportunities for children to solve their problems themselves and not to be manipulated or directed;
- to plan the intervention process at individual children's pace and not to be hurried;
- to establish essential limitations to keep children safe and within the world of reality.

Techniques discussed so far intend to 'cure the within child problem' and do not immediately change unacceptable behaviour to acceptable behaviour. Early-years professionals, however, often have to deal immediately with behaviours that may be harmful for both the individual child and the whole class. Therefore, they often need to act immediately and deal with overt or 'surface' behaviours (Charlton and David 1989). Techniques for 'surface' behaviour management include (Walker and Shea 1988):

- eye contact, frown and staring
- moving physically towards or standing near the misbehaving child
- ignoring misbehaviour
- maintaining routine, and providing additional materials and equipment
- programme restructuring
- removal of objects that may attract pupils' attention or distract them from the task
- removing the child from an activity when he or she becomes frustrated or upset
- giving a word of praise or positive comment about a task
- giving praise and affection that allows children to cope with anxiety
- adopting a sense of humour
- physical restraint, whenever necessary, to prevent children from harming themselves or others

Although the psychoeducational approach is based on the assumption that the problem resides within the individual, techniques discussed seem to present a multilevel orientation in dealing with children's problems. Expressive arts address children's inner world by encouraging and providing them opportunities to express indirectly negative feeling and emotions in an acceptable manner. Counselling allows children to talk through their difficulties and helps them to develop socially acceptable behaviours, while 'surface' behaviour management is used to deal with overt behaviour which interferes with daily functioning.

The behavioural approach

In the 1960s the behavioural approach gained credibility in dealing with behaviour problems in the school context. The behavioural approach is based on the central thesis of behaviourism which states that behaviour is acquired and maintained through learning explained in terms of reinforcement (McBurnett et al. 1989). The behavioural approach focuses on objectively observable behaviour rather than on any underlying disorder within the individual (Nelson and Rutherford Jr. 1988; Davie 1989). Furthermore, behaviour is studied in the context of the immediate environment and emphasis is placed in assessing current situational determinants of the behaviour, that is what has preceded and followed the behaviour identified (McBurnett et al. 1989; Levis 1990). Preceding events influence behaviour to the extent of enabling children to discriminate that certain consequences will follow certain behaviour (Kerr and Nelson 1989). Therefore, it is mainly the consequences or the probable consequences of the behaviour which actually control and reinforce the behaviour (Shea and Bauer 1988). Such consequences are known as reinforcers and constitute the main principle of the behavioural approach (Milan 1990).

The identification and selection of appropriate and potent reinforcers is of paramount importance in planning an intervention programme. Shea and Bauer (1987) claim that a behavioural approach is only as effective as its reinforcers. The effectiveness of any reinforcer is strongly determined by the extent to which it meets children's own feelings and needs. These needs may be made explicit by carefully observing children or by asking them about things they would like to have or do (Presland 1989; Kazdin 1990). Reinforcers are basically classified as tangible or primary reinforcers (e.g. food, drinks, tokens) and social or secondary reinforcers (e.g. signs of approval, praise, smiles). These categories of reinforcers also reflect the developmental nature of children's preference for rewards. Primitive and concrete reinforcers such as edible and tangible are mainly applied to younger children, while more abstract such as social reinforcers are often more appropriate for older children (Fantuzzo et al. 1991).

On the basis of this theoretical background, behaviourally oriented professionals have devised and implemented numerous intervention programmes, strategies and specific techniques which are classified into two major categories, that is behaviour enhancement procedures and behaviour reduction procedures (Nelson and Rutherford Jr. 1988; Kazdin 1990). In the behaviour enhancement procedures, rewarding techniques attempt to strengthen, maintain or increase the frequency of an appropriate behaviour. In the behaviour reduction procedures, punishing techniques are used to eliminate the frequency of inappropriate behaviour. Both behaviour enhancement and behaviour reduction have been found applicable in the classroom and across all group ages and all kinds of behaviour problems (Atwater and Morris 1988; Nelson and Rutherford Jr. 1988; Wheldall and Merrett 1992).

In general teachers tend to work on procedures and techniques that redirect pupils toward appropriate behaviour (Trovato et al. 1992). Social reinforcement in the form of approval and praise has been found as the most widely used and most effective technique followed by token economy. But the use of praise and token economy in conjunction seems to further reinforce appropriate behaviour (Cameron and Pierce 1994). Some researchers have reported mild punitive techniques to be effective, but generally punishment is considered as the least effective intervention. It results in the suppression of the undesirable behaviour at the time rather than in eliminating it in the long term (Levis 1990). It may teach children what not to do, but it does not provide any instruction in what they should do under the circumstances (Kaplan 1988). In particular, for young children, who often do not know what to do or how something must be done, punishment for mistakes may make things worse by bringing about anxiety and fear (Kazdin 1990; Meyhew 1997).

In terms of the behavioural approach teachers are a paramount variable in dealing with behaviour problems. Many of the behaviours which teachers find disruptive are actually within their control. Teachers can modify and control pupils' behaviour by controlling their own responses (Thomas et al. 1968). However, the behavioural approach becomes effective only if teachers apply specific techniques consistently, otherwise such techniques may become more confusing for both the child and the teacher. Indeed, it is not always easy for teachers who deal with thirty or even more children in a class to be consistent in applying these techniques. Techniques also are not easily acquired and most teachers find it difficult to be spontaneous and genuine in praising a child displaying behaviour problems. In many cases techniques appear to be time-consuming and interfere with teaching process and materials used as reinforcers can be expensive if they are used on a regular basis. Furthermore, sometimes teachers are reluctant to use the behavioural approach simply because it involves manipulation of children's own behaviour without their consent and often against their will (Fontana 1985). For this, the behavioural approach still remains a controversial issue in dealing with behaviour problems and many teachers seem to be reluctant in using it (Docking 1980; Nelson and Rutherford Jr. 1988).

The cognitive approach

By the 1970s researchers started to question the emphasis given to overt behaviour and shifted their interest to the study of cognitive concepts. Whilst they did not completely reject the behavioural approach, some of them who were influenced by the social learning theories came to adopt the cognitive approach. The cognitive approach places emphasis on how children cognitively structure their experience and approach situations and in particular on how they can modify incongruent cognition (Ingram and Scott 1990; Levis 1990). It is suggested that a change in cognition will result in changes in overt behaviour (Levis 1990). Nursery and primary school children, being at a developmental stage in which their cognition is not highly developed, often do not know what is acceptable or what is expected from them. Sometimes they are not even aware that their behaviour is irritating and disturbing. Teachers then tend to adopt interventions which emphasise the important role of cognition and cognitive processes in the manifestation and change of overt behaviour (Fontana 1985; Kagan and Smith 1988; Kazdin 1990; Levis 1990).

In devising cognitive strategies to deal with behaviour problems teachers must introduce certain rules to their pupils. Pupils must understand which aspects of their behaviour are perceived as unacceptable and why. They must be helped to see the consequences of their unacceptable behaviour and actions, but also helped to identify positive aspects of their behaviour and work towards realistic standards. Instructions, guidance, emphasising rationality, role-play and behaviour rehearsal are some of the cognitive techniques used by teachers in the classroom context. Instructions and guidance clearly state specific skills to be taught and rationales provide the reason for learning these skills. In both role-play and behaviour rehearsal pupils rehearse how to behave in situations which may cause difficulties (Fontana 1985; Morgan and Jenson 1988).

The cognitive approach emphasising only rationality tends to neglect emotions. However, current research has clearly shown that emotions constitute the basis of all rational actions. An understanding of the link between an event, its interpretation and the emotions that follow is an important key to deal with behaviour problems (Goleman 1996; Meyhew 1997; Wilks 1998). In the light of these views, the cognitive–affective theory has recently emerged. Affective variables such as feelings, thoughts and interpersonal relationships and the way they affect cognition have started to be studied and taken into account (Carpenter and Apter 1988; Ingram and Scott 1990). 'Affective' education and the 'self-control' curriculum constitute part of the cognitive–affective theory and they both have been designed to help pupils to increase awareness and understanding of personal emotions, values, and attitudes through educational activities. They include games, role play, lessons and discussion implemented in small, developmental steps, which provide positive feedback (Shea and Bauer 1987; Walker and Shea 1988).

Cognitive approaches actively employ cognitive processes for children's self-control of own behaviour as opposed to the external control of behaviour as it happens with the conventional behavioural approaches (Carpenter and Apter 1988). In general, these techniques aim to help children to develop skills for coping more effectively with problem-arousing situations, and adapt to stressful circumstances that are largely out of their control. They help children to increase their appraisal of information and learn new and effective ways of problem solving. Importantly, such techniques can be used to teach social behaviours and to alter children's irrational beliefs through logic and persuasion. Developing sensitivity to others and verbalising their feelings in certain situations in the hope that such experience will enable them to bring their behaviour under control is also advocated in this approach (Fontana 1985; Carpenter and Apter 1988; Elliot and Place 1998). Although some techniques used in the cognitive approach seem to overlap with those used in the psychoeducational approach, still the cognitive approach is broader in the sense that it aims to deal with both the causes of a problem and the particular symptoms exhibited. Cognitive techniques seem also to be nursery teachers' favourite techniques. Instructions, guidance, counselling, role-play and rehearsal are an essential part of any early-years curriculum and setting, and meeting young children's developmental needs have been found to be the most frequently used techniques in the nursery classroom (Papatheodorou 1995). The main objection for the cognitive approach is that it is vague, imprecise and subjective, mainly because it is not based on a particular theory. Individual teachers may give their own interpretations to children's problems, following an intervention plan they think is the most appropriate (Fontana 1985).

The ecosystemic approach

According to Molnar and Lindquist (1989), in an educational context teachers and their pupils are part of a classroom ecosystem and therefore are influenced by the ecosystemic relations in that classroom. Behaviour, in ecological terms, is seen as a function of ongoing dynamic interrelationships between the individual and the environment rather than residing either within the individual or the environment (Cooper and Upton 1990;1992). Behaviour problems may reflect an interplay of nature–nurture, but all have an interactional/relational component (Talay-Ongan 1998). The school ecosystem consists of the pupils themselves and all those events that might affect pupils' behaviour at any given point in time. However, the role of individuals' perceptions and interpretations of any given situation are strongly emphasised in the ecosystemic approach. The assumption that individuals behave according to the way in which they interpret the situation becomes its basic principle. Often there is more than one valid interpretation for any particular situation. Therefore changing the interpretation will lead to a change in behaviour. In turn such changes in behaviour will influence others' perceptions and behaviour (Molnar and Lindquist 1989; Cooper and Upton 1992; Conoley and Carrington Rotto 1997).

Ecosystemic techniques are based on the principle of 'reframing' or 'divergent explanations of problem behaviour'. It is suggested that teachers should re-examine specific problematic situations by redefining behaviour problems, self-evaluate their own reactions to this behaviour and consider what purpose the behaviour serves for the pupil (Molnar and Lindquist 1989; Conoley and Carrington Rotto 1997). An empathetic understanding then becomes the key feature in the ecosystemic approach. The use of empathy may help teachers to continually analyse the experience of schooling from the pupil's point of view. As Purkey and Novak point out that what may be seen as illogical 'from an external point of view is only an inadequate understanding of what the world looks like from the internal viewpoint of the behaving person' (1984: 32). Importantly Zabel (1988) points out that approaching behaviour problems in this way requires teachers who themselves have achieved a high degree of maturity, who are well-adjusted, warm, objective and supportive.

Ecosystemic techniques are not addressed to individual children only but to the whole system/school in which behaviour problems are exhibited. Teachers' understanding of how context events affect behaviour may provide important information on the basis of which intervention will then be planned, and provide important guidance for preventing or avoiding an unexpected crisis (Cooper and Upton 1990; 1992; Conoley and Carrington Rotto 1997). In the light of these assumptions, a whole-school approach in dealing with children's problems has been developed. This approach focuses on the whole-school context and involves a radical examination of what schools offer to all children and staff. It is responsive and supportive to the needs of both, and incorporates help from parents and the community (Burden 1992; O'Brien 1998; Wilson 1998).

At a theoretical level the ecosystemic approach seems to be more promising in dealing with behaviour problems, but there is little research support for its effectiveness. The conceptualisation of children's behaviour problems and relevant management approaches remain a proposed synthesis which needs to be further studied. However, the ecosystemic approach seems to provide a valuable addition to what has already been achieved by other behaviour management approaches (Cooper and Upton 1992).

Conclusion

For more than four decades now there has been evidence of a movement from a purely psychoeducational approach, which mainly addresses within-the-child causes, to a behavioural approach, which addresses environmental stimuli. The behavioural approach however has tended to ignore children's cognition and feelings and has not taken into account the multi-faceted nature of behaviour problems, which, according to the ecological theory, are largely determined by the dynamic interaction processes between all parts involved within a particular ecosystem. Both cognitive and ecosystemic approaches have made important contributions to these issues.

However, teachers seem not to be theory-oriented. They tend to employ and use whatever techniques have been proved to be effective and work in their particular situation with their particular pupils. In general they use positive ways to deal with children's behaviour problems, but they do deliver punishment as well. The ease with which management techniques can be applied in the classroom and the extent to which they meet children's developmental needs seem also to affect teachers' decisions about their employment. Teachers also tend to avoid techniques that are complicated, time-consuming and require extra material for their application, as often happens with the behavioural techniques (Schneider et al. 1992). In general they tend to employ a variety of techniques of different theoretical orientation, indicating that their eclecticism is effect rather than theory oriented (Papatheodorou 1995).

Teachers' eclecticism with regard to behaviour management techniques is likely to be an advantage as long as teachers do not allow one approach to confuse or contradict the other, either in their own eyes or in those of their pupils (Fontana 1985). Indeed, such eclecticism seems to indicate that an integrated perspective which would consider both pupils' and teachers' experiences, and school pragmatics, would be more promising than any approach discussed alone. The ecosystemic approach appears to present the framework where such eclecticism can have its place. Psychoeducational, behavioural and cognitive techniques can all be part of the ecosystemic approach and they can address problems at different levels of functioning. However, professionals must bear in mind that the approaches and techniques which they use need to be consistent with and reflect the way they conceptualise and understand children's behaviour problems. Professionals need to be clear why they use the techniques they do use. This point becomes particularly important for the early-years professionals who are called to play a vital role in the early identification and management of young children's behaviour problems (DfEE 1997; 1998).

References

Atwater, J. and Morris, E. (1989) 'Teachers' Instructions and Children's Compliance in Pre-school Classrooms: A Descriptive Analysis', *Journal of Applied Behavior Analysis* 21(2): 157–167.

Axline, V. (1989) *Play Therapy*, Edinburgh: Churchill Livingstone.

Burden, R. (1992) 'Whole-school Approaches to Disruption: What Part Can Psychology Play?' in K. Wheldall (ed.) *Discipline in Schools, Psychological Perspectives on the Elton Report*, London: Routledge.

Cameron, J. and Pierce, W. (1994) 'Reinforcement, Reward and Intrinsic Motivation: A Meta-Analysis', *Review of Educational Research* 64(3): 363–423.

Carpenter, R. and Apter, S. (1988) 'Research Integration of Cognitive-Emotional Interventions for Behaviorally Disordered Children and Youth', in M. Wang, M. Reynolds, and H. Walberg (eds) *Handbook of Special Education Research and Practice*, Vol.2 Oxford: Pergamon Press.

Charlton, T. and David, T. (1989) 'Reflection and Implications', in T. Charlton and T. David (eds) *Managing Misbehaviour. Strategies for Effective Management of Behaviour in Schools*, Basingstoke: Macmillan.

Conoley, J. and Carrington Rotto, P. (1997) 'Ecological Interventions with students', in J. Swartz and W. Martin (eds) *Applied Ecological Psychology for Schools Within Communities. Assessment and Intervention*, Mahwah, NJ: Lawrence Erlbaum.

Cooper, P. and Upton, G. (1990) 'An Ecosystemic Approach to Emotional and Behavioural Difficulties in Schools', *Educational Psychology*, 10(4): 301–321.

—— (1992) 'An Ecosystemic Approach to Classroom Behaviour Problems', in K. Wheldall (ed.) *Discipline in Schools. Psychological Perspectives on the Elton Report*, London: Routledge.

Davie, R. (1986) 'Understanding Behaviour Problems', *Maladjustment and Therapeutic Education* 4(1): 2–11.

Davie, R. (1989) 'Behaviour Problems and the Teacher', in T. Charlton and K. David (eds) *Managing Misbehaviour. Strategies for Effective Management of Behaviour in Schools*, Basingstoke and London: Macmillan Education.

DfEE (1997) *Excellence for All Children. Meeting Special Educational Needs* (Green Paper), Sudbury: DfEE Publications.

—— (1998) *Meeting Special Educational Needs. A Programme for Action* (White Paper), Sudbury: DfEE Publications.

Docking, S. (1980) *Control and Discipline in Schools. Perspectives and Approaches*, London: Harper and Row.

Elliot, J. and Place, M. (1998) *Children in Difficulty. A Guide to Understanding and Helping*, London: Routledge.

Fantuzzo, J., Bohrbeck, C., Hightower, A., and Work, W. (1991) 'Teachers' Use and Children's Preferences of Rewards in Elementary School', *Psychology in the Schools* **28**: 175–181.

Fontana, D. (1985) *Classroom Control*, Leicester: British Psychological Society.

Goleman, D.(1996) *Emotional Intelligence*, London: Bloomsbury.

Ingram, R. and Scott, W. (1990) 'Cognitive Behavior Therapy', in A.S. Bellack, M. Hersen, and A. Kazdin (eds) *International Handbook of Behavior Modification and Therapy*, New York: Plenum.

Kagan, D. and Smith, K. (1988) 'Beliefs and Behaviors of Kindergarten Teachers', *Educational Research* **30**(1): 26–35.

Kaplan, P. (1988) *The Human Odyssey. Life-Span Development*, USA: West Publishing

Kazdin, A. (1990) 'Conduct Disorders', in A. Bellack, M. Hersen and A. Kazdin (eds) *International Handbook of Behavior Modification and Therapy*, New York: Plenum.

Kerr, M. and Nelson, M. (1989) *Strategies for Managing Behavior Problems in the Classroom*, Columbus: Merrill Publishing Co.

Lavoritano, J. and Segal, P. (1992) 'Evaluating the Efficacy of a School Counselling Program', *Psychology in the Schools* **29**: 61–70.

Levis, D. (1990) 'The Experimental and Theoretical Foundations of Behavior Modification', in A. Bellack, M. Hersen, and A. Kazdin, (eds) *International Handbook of Behavior Modification and Therapy*, New York: Plenum.

Mayhew, J. (1997) *Psychological Change. A Practical Introduction*, Basingstoke and London: Macmillan.

McBurnett, K., Hobbs, S. and Lahey, B. (1989) 'Behavioral Treatment', in T. Ollendick and M. Hersen (eds) *Handbook of Child Psychopathology*, New York: Plenum Press.

Milan, M. (1990) 'Applied Behavior Analysis', in A. Bellack, M. Hersen and A. Kazdin (eds) *International Handbook of Behavior Modification and Therapy*, New York: Plenum Press.

Molnar, A. and Lindquist, B. (1989) *Changing Behavior in Schools*, San Francisco, CA: Jossey Bass Publishers.

Morgan, D. and Jenson, W. (1988) *Teaching Behaviorally Disordered Students*, Colombus: Merril Publishing.

Murgatroyd, S. (1985) *Counselling and Helping*, Leicester: British Psychological Society.

Nelson, C. and Rutherford, Jnr., R. (1988) 'Behavioral Interventions with Behaviorally Disordered Students', in M. Wang, M. Reynolds and H. Walberg (eds) *Handbook of Special Education. Research and Practice. Mildly Handicapped Conditions*, vol.2, Oxford: Pergamon Press.

O'Brien, T. (1998) *Promoting Positive Behaviour*, London: David Fulton Publishers.

Papatheodorou, T. (1995) *Teachers' Attitudes toward Children's Behaviour Problems in Nursery Classes in Greece and the Management Techniques Used*, unpublished Ph.D. thesis. University of Wales College of Cardiff.

Presland, S. (1989) 'Behavioural Approaches', in T. Charlton and T. David (eds) *Managing Misbehaviour. Strategies for Effective Management of Behaviour in Schools*, Basingstoke: Macmillan.

Purkey, W. and Novak, J. (1984) *Inviting School Success: A Self-Concept Approach To Teaching and Learning*, Belmont, CA: Wadsworth Publishing Co.

Rhodes, W. (1974) 'An Overview:Towards a Synthesis of Models of Disturbance', in W. Rhodes and M. Tracy (eds) *A Study of Child Variance*, vol.1 *Conceptual Models*, Ann Arbor, MI: The University of Michigan Press.

Schneider, B., Kerridge, A. and Katz, J. (1992) 'Teacher Acceptance of Psychological Interventions of Varying Theoretical Orientation', *School Psychology International*, 13: 291–305.

Shea, T. and Bauer, A. (1987) *Teaching Children and Youth with Behavior Disorders*, Englewood Cliffs, NJ: Prentice Hall.

Talay-Ongan, A. (1998) *Typical and Atypical Development in Early Childhood: The Fundamentals*, Leicester: British Psychological Society.

Thomas, D., Becker, W. and Armsrong, M. (1968) 'Production and Elimination of Disruptive Classroom Behavior by Systematically Varying Teachers' Behavior', *Journal of Applied Behavior Analysis* 1(1): 35–45.

Trovato, J., Harris, J., Pryor, C. and Wilkinson, S. (1992) 'Teachers in Regular Classrooms: An Appplied Setting for Successful Behavior Programming', *Psychology in the Schools* 29: 52–61.

Walker, J. and Shea, T. (1988) *Behaviour Management. A Practical Approach for Educators*, Colombus: Merrill Publishing.

Wheldall, K. and Merrett, F. (1992) 'Effective Classroom Behaviour Management: Positive Teaching', in K. Wheldall (ed.) *Discipline in Schools. Psychological Perspectives on the Elton Report*, London: Routledge.

Wilks, F. (1998) *Intelligent Emotion. How to Succeed Through Transforming Your Feelings*, London: W.Heinmans.

Wilson, R. (1998) *Special Educational Needs in the Early Years*, London: Routledge.

Zabel, R. (1988) 'Preparation of Teachers for Behaviorally Disordered Students: A Review of Literature', in M. Wang, M. Reynolds and H. Walberg (eds) *Handbook of Special Education. Research and Practice*, vol.2, Oxford: Pergamon Press.

Chapter 10

Early intervention for hearing-impaired children in families of ethnic minority origin

Susan Turner and Wendy Lynas

Introduction

> They told me Imran was very deaf – he could only hear very loud noises such as big lorries passing or people shouting close by him. They said it wasn't the sort of deafness a lot of children get – the kind that comes and goes when they have colds. Our son's deafness is permanent. Will he ever talk? How will he ever understand us? Will he speak our language [Punjabi]? Will he learn English? Will he have to go to a special school? Will he be taken away from his family, his culture, his religion? Who is going to help us? What strangers will come to our home? Will we understand them?

This mother had been given the diagnosis of sensori-neural deafness in her child – a condition which affects approximately one in every thousand children in the general population (Newton 1985; Davis and Wood 1992). The anxieties of Imran's mother arise from her fear that without normal hearing, Imran will not learn to talk like other children. Like all parents of deaf children, she foresees all kinds of difficulties which may follow from her child's communication problem. She also sees that for her child the difficulties are exacerbated because the family's cultural background and their home language are unlike those of most other deaf children and unlike those of the professional workers who provide services to help them. Professional workers, for their part, share a concern that they may not be able to provide effective support for families where language and culture differ from their own.

Concern about service provision to ethnic minority families with young deaf children led to a research study based at the University of Manchester in 1995–7. The study sought to assess the proportion of young deaf children who were from ethnic minority homes, the proportion who did not have English as the predominant language of the home and the quality of the provision which aimed to help the families to meet their children's special needs. In this chapter we give an account of the research study and its findings. We set these findings in the context of the work of education services for hearing-impaired children with children under five and their families.

The research study

The research study began with a survey of all education services for hearing-impaired children in England. The 92 per cent response confirmed earlier regional findings about the high proportion of Asian children in the deaf population (Vanniasegaram, Tungland and Bellman 1993; Fortnum and Davis 1997; Naeem and Newton 1996). The 98 responding services were supporting a total of 2118 deaf children under five; 18.8 per cent of these children were from ethnic minority groupings; 12.2 per cent of the total were from South Asian families (Indian, Bangladeshi and Pakistani). According to the 1991 Census, only 6 per cent of the general population are from ethnic minority groupings and 3 per cent are South Asians (Owen 1992). It was thus clear that there were 3–4 times as many South Asian deaf children under five as would be expected from the proportion in the general population. The survey showed the proportion of deaf children from ethnic minority families to be higher in urban than in rural areas. In some of the inner London boroughs, more than 50 per cent of the deaf children under five were from ethnic minority families. The survey also found that more than half the ethnic minority families (13 per cent of the total) did not have English as the predominant language of the home, South Asians making up the greater part of this percentage (over 10 per cent of the total).

The second part of the research study was a series of interviews with teachers of the deaf in eight different local authorities in England (London boroughs, urban areas outside London and county areas). In these interviews, resources and good practice in meeting the specific needs of ethnic minority deaf children were discussed. The discussions focused on how intervention for ethnic minority families, when provided by white British professionals,[1] can avoid the charge of institutional racism i.e. being a service designed for the white majority which takes no account of cultural differences (Baxter et al. 1990).

Early intervention

To put the findings of these discussions into context we should explain that 'support' for deaf children and their families is undertaken primarily by peripatetic teachers of the deaf. They are teachers who have an additional qualification in the education of deaf children. Their support begins as soon as the diagnosis of hearing loss is confirmed at the audiology clinic. For 'at risk' babies this may be when they are just a month old since babies can now be tested initially within a few days of their birth. For other children, the diagnosis may follow the routine 'distraction' test of hearing by health visitors when the baby is old enough to sit up securely at about 8 months. Sometimes it still happens that deafness is not

---

[1] There are some Asian teachers of the deaf. Precise numbers are not known but are certainly very low. In the eight services for this study, all the teachers interviewed were white British.

identified until a child is at nursery or school. This may be because the deafness was not present in the child's first years or it may be that early test appointments were missed or that the tests failed to detect the hearing loss. Whatever the age of the child at diagnosis, the parents must face the fact that they have a new and difficult task: they have to learn about the nature of their child's impairment and they also have to acquire new skills so that they are able to manage his or her newly discovered needs.

The peripatetic teacher of the deaf has a very complex and delicate task. She has to help the adults in the family to understand their child's hearing loss and its implications.[2] This part of her work varies according to whether there is any previous experience of deafness and according to the family's willingness and ability to learn. The teacher of the deaf has to support parents (and other carers) in consistent use of the hearing aids and to discuss with them strategies which will help the child to develop communication skills. She must keep them informed about all locally available resources including those of voluntary agencies such as the National Deaf Children's Society. She may invite parents to meet with others in groups either for social occasions or for a specific purpose such as a signing class or a music session to which parents bring their young deaf children. The peripatetic teacher's work also includes counselling since parents are often shocked, angry or even in denial about their child's deafness (Luterman 1987). They need someone to talk to who understands childhood deafness and who is prepared to listen to their reactions and their worries about the future. The teacher of the deaf must balance the child's need for making the best possible use of the vital early years for language development (through use of the hearing aids and linguistic stimulation) with that of allowing parents to work through their negative reactions to the diagnosis and to retain control of their child. She must avoid suggesting any deficit in parenting skills while at the same time making clear that the child has certain very specific needs which must be met if the child is to realise his or her potential (Sandow 1990).

The teacher brings specialist expertise and parents bring knowledge of their child and together they must decide strategies for working with the deaf child (Dale 1996).

Intervention for the child in an ethnic minority family

Early intervention for a deaf child is thus never an easy task but the research showed that where there are cultural and linguistic differences between professional and family, the difficulties can be much greater. For example, the teacher of the deaf has expertise and experience of the way in which sharing everyday

---

[2] More women than men undertake training as teachers of the deaf and it is usually women, rather than men, who make home visits to families of pre-school deaf children.

activities with the child helps their development of language. However, if the teacher is uncertain about normal childcare practice and domestic routine in the Asian home, how is she to suggest involving the child in these activities? The teacher may want to recommend that adults in the family use play activities to help the child but if such activities are not part of their normal practice, as some of the teachers interviewed maintained, does it make sense for her to encourage the use of toys and play activities with the deaf child?

Not only domestic routine but also family dynamics are likely to differ in some ethnic minority households. British health and education services, and indeed legislation such as the Children Act, 1989, tend to assume that a child's parents have sole responsibility for any decisions relating to the child. However, in other cultures, grandparents and other senior relatives may have a degree of authority rarely seen in a white British family. A family's expectations for their child may also be different from those in white British families. For example, working towards independence for the child may be less important in an Asian family than helping him or her to become a dependable member of the extended family. Teachers of the deaf thus have to be prepared to include all adult members of the family in the support they offer and they cannot base suggestions to aid the child's development on the assumption that all parents want their child to become more independent (Dwivedi 1996).

In discussion about the child's development of language, the issue of modes of communication has to be raised. This is a vexed question for professionals and one which is presented to many parents soon after the child's diagnosis. Parents have the right to choose whether their child should have sign or speech as their main mode of communication. However, the issues of whether to use sign or an auditory–oral approach for a deaf child are very complex and making an informed choice is extremely difficult for most parents who have no previous experience of deafness. Moreover, while professionals try to offer unbiased information, the policy of each service and the preferences of each professional can make it hard to avoid prejudicing the decision for parents (Lynas 1994). Where parents have a different cultural and/or linguistic background from that of the professionals, fully-informed choice is even harder to ensure.

When their choice of mode of communication is made, there are fresh demands on families. If signing is to be used, it is essential that the family learn to sign. For families who speak a minority language at home, this means learning a third language. They must attend sign language classes – not easy for any parents but for women who, for cultural reasons, will not use public transport unescorted, it may be impossible for them to get to the classes. The teacher of sign language is usually a deaf person and is unlikely to know any other minority language. If an interpreter is used in the classes, there will have to be translation from sign to English and then from English to the minority language. In some parent groups it would be necessary to have more than one minority language interpreter. Funding for interpreters' services is not always available.

Parents who opt for spoken language for the child have to decide whether to use their own language or to speak English with their child. Parents may decide that speaking English will simplify language acquisition for the child but it carries the risk of isolating him or her if the family normally speak another language (Ahmad, Darr, Jones and Nisar 1998). Moreover, if the child's main care-givers speak English with difficulty, they may provide poor models of language to the child. If parents decide to use their own language, the teacher who only speaks English will not be able to give direct linguistic help to the child. There is also the problem for the child of starting school with perhaps a limited amount of the family's language and no English at all. If parents feel that the child should learn two spoken languages, how is this to be achieved when, because of deafness, competence in one presents major difficulties to the child (Chamba, Ahmad and Jones 1998)?

Issues about language, use of hearing aids and prospects for a deaf child are all very complex and for honest discussion and genuine partnership it is essential that the teacher of the deaf and the parents understand each other. In most families, the mother is the primary care-giver and it is mainly with her that the teacher of the deaf has to discuss the needs of the deaf child. However, in many ethnic minority homes, the mother has less fluent English than the father and an exchange of ideas and questions, expression of beliefs and principles may be very difficult for both mother and teacher. In some cases interpreters may be employed to help the process of mutual understanding. However, interpreters are costly and they may not be available for all home visits. Even when interpreters are available, there can be problems in discussing complex or subtle issues. As one of the teachers interviewed commented, it is hard to express subtle shades of meaning or any emotion through an interpreter and unless you are used to working with a particular interpreter, you may not be certain that the interpretation is accurate.

The management of hearing aids must be explained to all parents of deaf children. Hearing aids are fitted soon after the diagnosis is confirmed and an initial explanation of how they work is given to the parents. However, understanding the technical complexity of the many small parts of a hearing aid and ensuring that it is in full working order at all times is daunting to every parent. For parents whose first language is not English, the problems of understanding hearing aid management are likely to be enhanced.

Ensuring that parents understand the need for consistent use of hearing aids is another important task for the teacher of the deaf. Not all babies take to hearing aids immediately and by no means all parents like their child to be seen wearing them. For some ethnic minority families there are cultural objections to hearing aids. These objections may not be expressed to the teacher and when they are, she may not appreciate them. The relationship of trust and partnership which depends largely on being able to communicate freely, has to be well established for such matters to be openly discussed and resolved.

The teacher of the deaf also has to discuss with parents whether the child should have a cochlear implant. This is a surgical procedure to implant an electrical device into the inner ear which restores a certain amount of hearing to profoundly deaf people. It is increasingly being offered to very deaf children from the age of about two years. It involves not only surgery but many hospital visits before and after the operation for scans, assessments, discussions and post-operative programming of the device. Cochlear implants do not restore hearing to normal but they do raise the level of hearing so that the child has a greatly improved chance of acquiring spoken language. Here again, problems may arise for the minority family both with regard to the language for explaining cochlear implantation and with the logistics of getting to and from the hospital for appointments (Archbold and Robinson 1997). Some children in ethnic minority families have now had cochlear implants but research into the ethnicity of child implantees in all thirteen cochlear implant centres in the UK showed that there were disproportionately few children from ethnic minority groups (Jamieson 1998). It is relevant to ask why there is this racial disproportion and whether the small number of ethnic minority children who are benefiting from cochlear implantation is an indication of indirect racism.

The study included questions about minority families' participation in parent group meetings – these are organised by services for hearing-impaired children or by local deaf children's societies. Not all parents want to meet other families simply because they have deaf children in common but for many they are a great source of mutual support and a way of learning more about meeting their own child's needs. However, in many areas, getting to the meeting place involves journeys by bus or car. For people with other family commitments this can be difficult and for others, as noted above, cultural practice prevents their travelling alone on public transport.

As we have noted, effective early intervention is achieved in the context of parent–professional partnership. However, in the culture of some communities, the professional person is seen as the 'expert' and although parents want what is best for their child they may not feel that their own views should carry any weight in deciding exactly what is 'best'. Teachers of the deaf interviewed for the research study appreciated the hospitality and the respect shown by families they visited but sometimes they had difficulties in persuading ethnic minority parents to be confident of their own expertise and knowledge of their child.

In summary, the issues which add to the complexity of early intervention for ethnic minority families with a hearing-impaired child include:

- the process of building a parent–professional relationship with people of a different cultural background especially where there are language differences;
- cultural differences which may affect the consistent use and management of hearing aids;
- teachers' lack of understanding of normal childcare, domestic routine and expectations for the child in ethnic minority families;
- teachers' lack of understanding of family dynamics such as deference to senior family members and differences in the role of women;

- linguistic problems when trying to explain complex issues (such as modes of communication, management of hearing aids and cochlear implants) even when interpreters are available to help;
- obtaining interpreters when they are needed, training them with regard to the subject matter and learning to work with them;
- helping parents to decide about the use of English and/or the language of the home;
- helping the child to make progress in acquiring the home language if this is the parents' choice;
- helping parents to learn to sign, if signing is their choice for the child;
- enabling parents in ethnic minority groupings to attend meetings for sign classes or for mutual support;
- helping parents to be confident in their own expertise of knowing what is best for their child and to accept their role as partners with the teacher.

Resources and good practice

Not all the issues mentioned above were problems for all ethnic minority families being supported by teachers interviewed for the research study. For example, many ethnic minority parents have been born and educated in the UK and so have fluent English. Others have sufficient English for most purposes and may only need an interpreter occasionally. The different family dynamics and expectations usually (although not always) meant that families were more stable than white British families. Parents benefited from the support of older relatives: all the family were there to support what was best for the child. Moreover, because very few Pakistani and Bangladeshi mothers work outside the home (Modood 1997), they were available for home visits during the day and it was they, not child-minders, who cared for the children.

In some local authorities there were resources which went a long way towards making the service appropriate to families of every ethnic group. For example, in one area with a high proportion of Bangladeshi people in the population, a bilingual assistant had been appointed to work full-time with the service for hearing-impaired children. She went with the teacher of the deaf on home visits to interpret and in time she did some home visits on her own. She was able to interpret for the white British teachers not only the language but also the cultural background of the Bangladeshi families. This allowed the expertise of the teacher of the deaf to be offered to the parents of deaf children in the most meaningful way. In this same area the bilingual assistant could talk to the deaf child in the home language so demonstrating that the community language is valued.

In other local authorities the appointment of a single full-time bilingual assistant was not believed to be feasible because of lower numbers of ethnic minority deaf children and the variety of linguistic groups. However, teachers in some services for hearing-impaired children were able to call on specific interpreters who gradually built up experience of working with the service and understanding of the topics likely to be discussed. Where an interpreter was needed for a less common language it was considered essential to have time with the interpreter in advance of the session with parents.

Another strategy that was employed to overcome language barriers was to use family members as interpreters – some teachers said that this gave continuity but there could be problems in being sure that the interpretation was accurate. Shah (1995) is critical of this practice because of possible biases and power relationships in the family. On the positive side, however, it was a common experience among the teachers of the deaf for communication with parents and other family members to be difficult at first but to improve with time. Weekly home visits enabled mutual linguistic comprehension to develop at the same time as parents' understanding of the child's needs with regard to the hearing loss and the teacher's understanding of the child's needs in this particular family setting. There was no shortage of commitment on the part of the teachers interviewed to understand and to be understood: both family and teachers shared a deep concern for the deaf child and this in itself went a long way to promote mutual understanding and respect.

Some teachers reported the invaluable work done by 'link workers'. These were bilingual workers, sometimes appointed jointly by health and education authorities. They helped people in ethnic minority families to understand and to keep appointments and were sometimes available to give family support.

The link workers were an example of liaison between services run by health and education authorities. Good liaison was also common between education services for hearing-impaired children and the audiological services which are run by health authorities and trusts. Referral from audiological clinics to the education services was reported generally to be swift and teachers of the deaf could contribute valuable observations on the child's audiological responses in the home to help the audiologist in the task of making a full assessment of the child's hearing status and their use of amplification.

Many of the resources needed to make service provision appropriate to all families are costly. Local authorities have to be fully committed to the principle of equal opportunities if they are to release funds to put the principle into practice. A good example of such commitment was those authorities who would provide transport to enable parents to get to the venue for group meetings. Such provision of transport to the meeting venue was often crucial to their success. Some services reported that they were allowed funds to use local authority minibuses for this purpose.

Conclusion

The good practice which this study demonstrated can be summed up as determination on the part of teachers of the deaf to work for the best interests of each individual child and family in a relationship of parent–professional partnership. Parents were recognised as the most important people in a child's life and, for a deaf child, the empowerment of all parents to meet their child's needs was the key target of early intervention.

The teachers' concern about differences between their own cultural background and that of some of the families they were supporting was proof of their lack of complacency. None of the teachers interviewed believed that they had nothing to learn about the families they supported. Many admitted that they had started from a position of ignorance but had gained insight into cultural differences in the course of their work with ethnic minority families.

The lack of resources such as the shortage of interpreters and link workers is a very serious problem. Powers (1996) gives ethnicity, particularly when the child is from a minority language home, as an important factor in explaining the under-achievement of some deaf children in their GCSE results. If ethnic minority parents were better equipped to understand their young children's hearing loss in the early stages there would be a better chance of their children fully accessing educational opportunities later.

Ideally, early intervention would be undertaken by teachers of the deaf of the same ethnicity as the families they visit. Unfortunately, this is not a resource that can easily be created. Another resource, which was spoken about but which was not yet available, was video material in minority languages to help minority parents to understand their child's impairment and to portray some of the strategies which would help them to make progress.

Where there are bilingual assistants and link workers, they can transform the effectiveness of early intervention with ethnic minority families. If resources were available to allow more such appointments, to make good quality video material and enable more qualified ethnic minority teachers to undertake training as teachers of the deaf, there would undoubtedly be more ethnic minority parents who were well equipped with the necessary skills and knowledge to enable their deaf children to develop to their full potential.

References

Ahmad, W., Darr, A., Jones, L. and Nisar, G. (1998) *Deafness and Ethnicity: Services, Policy and Politics*, Bristol: Policy Press.

Archbold, S. and Robinson, K. (1997) 'Cochlear implantation, associated rehabilitation services and their educational implications: the UK and Europe', *Deafness and Education (Journal of the British Association of Teachers of the Deaf)* 21(1): 34–41.

Baxter, C., Poonia, K. Ward, L. and Nadirshaw, Z. (1990) *Double Discrimination: Issues and Services for People with Learning Difficulties from Black and Ethnic Minority Communities*, London: King's Fund Centre and Commission for Racial Equality.

Chamba, R., Ahmad, W. and Jones, L. (1998) *Improving services for Asian deaf children. Parents' and professionals' perspectives*, Bristol: Policy Press

Children Act (1989) London: HMSO.

Dale, N. (1996) *Working with Families of Children with Special Needs*, London and New York: Routledge.

Davis, A. and Wood, S. (1992) 'The epidemiology of childhood hearing impairment. Factors relevant to planning of services', *British Journal of Audiology* 26(2): 77–90.

Dwivedi, K. (1996) 'Culture and Personality', in K. Dwivedi and V. Varma (eds) *Meeting the Needs of Ethnic Minority Children: a Handbook for Professionals*, London: Jessica Kingsley Publishers.

Fortnum, H. and Davis, A. (1997) 'Epidemiology of permanent childhood hearing impairment in the Trent region, 1985–1993', *British Journal of Audiology* 31(6): 409–46.

Jamieson, L. (1998) *Cochlear Implants and Asian Families*, Paper to British Association of the Deaf (North Region) Conference.

Luterman, D. (1987) *Deafness in the Family*, Boston: Little, Brown & Co.

Lynas, W. (1994) 'Choosing between education options in the education of deaf children', *Journal of the British Association of Teachers of the Deaf* 18(5): 119–29.

Modood, T. (1997) 'Employment', in T. Modood and R. Berthoud (eds) *Ethnic Minorities in Britain: Diversity and Disadvantage*, London: Policy Studies Institute.

Naeem, Z. and Newton, V. (1996) 'Prevalence of sensori-neural hearing loss in Asian children', *British Journal of Audiology* 30(5): 332–9.

Newton, V. (1985) 'Aetiology of bi-lateral sensori-neural hearing loss in young children', *Journal of Laryngology and Otology* 99: Supplement 10.

Owen, D. (1992) *Ethnic Minorities in Great Britain: Settlement Patterns. 1991 Census Statistical Paper No. 1*, Coventry: Centre for Research in Ethnic Relations.

Powers, S. (1996) 'Deaf pupils' achievements in ordinary schools', *Journal of the British Association of Teachers of the Deaf* 20(4): 111–23.

Sandow, S. (1990) 'The Pre-School years: Early intervention and prevention', in P. Evans and V. Varma (eds) *Special Education Past, Present and Future*, London: Falmer Press.

Shah, R. (1995) *The Silent Minority*, London: National Children's Bureau.

Vanniasegaram, I., Tungland, O. and Bellman, S. (1993) 'A five year review of children with deafness in a multi-ethnic community', *Journal of Audiological Medicine* 2: 9–19.

Chapter 11

A contextual orientation to assessment

Andrew Lockett

Introduction

In this chapter, an emerging contextual orientation to assessing pre-school children with special educational needs is presented. The two aspects of the child's familiar context, and the problems arising from gathering differing viewpoints of all those in involved in that context, are explored.

When I was a teacher within a mainstream nursery context about 12 years ago, I observed children learning through play, and gathered information from all sources, including the parents, in order to understand their individual needs. I used that information to both review my own practice and to formulate curriculum plans. Children entering the nursery who caused concern, encouraged my nursery nurse and me to reflect upon our practice and to seek ways to adjust our teaching approaches and/or presentation of curricula experiences in order to enable all children to have access to the learning opportunities provided.

On one occasion, a child causing concern to us was referred to the Educational Psychological Service for assessment of her special educational needs. She was removed from the class context for the assessment, which took place at the local Child Development Centre. We were rather surprised at this withdrawal. The report that followed appeared to indicate that the child was less able than we knew her to be. Shortly following that assessment, some support workers from the Child Development Centre appeared in class with a box of activities to be carried out with the child, which were related to helping her discriminate between letters of the alphabet. This was not particularly helpful to us, as we ourselves needed to understand the needs of the child in order to inform our planning and adjust our teaching approaches.

This different stance being taken by professionals in the field of special educational needs caused us to question our approach. It seemed as if they viewed the child as the root of a special needs problem. As a result, the curriculum planned for that child was narrowed and ordered sequentially, and the teaching appeared to be seen more as a technical activity of teaching developmentally appropriate skills.

Importance of context

This episode began an investigation into the underlying principles that guided my developing approach to assessment. The context within which a child with special educational needs was learning was of paramount importance. This view was further re-enforced in my role as an early-years support teacher. I used to attend the senior clinical medical officer's clinic, or observed the educational psychologists administering assessment tasks within a quiet area withdrawn from an early-years setting. What I observed was children performing well below what I knew they could do within the normal routine of their familiar context.

On one such occasion, a child would not co-operate with one single task that a Senior Medical Officer attempted to carry out, and under-functioned. The stress of the situation in unfamiliar surroundings with an unfamiliar adult was more than the child could cope with. In the home context, I knew that many of the tasks could be completed fairly successfully if presented at an appropriate time.

Such experiences supported the view that assessments should be carried out within a child's familiar context. The practice of observing children in the home context became part of my normal practice. On many occasions a home teaching programme was followed. The programme of learning took on the form of developmentally appropriate range of skills to be taught sequentially. It was a mother of a child I was visiting regularly, who was a nursery nurse prior to raising a family, who questioned the approach being taken, and argued for support to adjust her everyday interactions and planning of experiences to meet the needs of the child in question.

As I reflected on such encounters, was there not a parallel here with the support workers who came into my nursery class and prescribed activities that did not support or help me in adjusting my interactions and teaching approaches? Was I not just as guilty as those professionals several years before?

This led to a different orientation to assessment emerging. I began to consider the child within his or her teaching and learning context, and to consider how to support the parents, carers and other adults in acquiring observational skills, in interpreting those observations in order to support the planning of experiences and make adjustments in their styles of interaction, both verbally and through play.

The work of Heshusius (1991) and Bronfenbrenner (1979) influenced my thinking in regards to developing the importance of the context or ecology of assessment. The 'Whole Language Movement' described by Goodman (1978) stresses the importance of all aspects of the child's context for learning. It is by adopting more holistic approaches to gathering data from the child's familiar teaching and learning context, that I believe the child and teaching pedagogy become balanced in considering how to promote learning more effectively.

Assessing contextually in education

Whilst working as an Advisory Teacher for Special Educational Needs I began to elaborate a contextual approach to assessing the special educational needs of preschool children, through the compilation of a case study.

The approach formulated was based upon a problem-solving model in the tradition of action research (Elliott 1976). The approach contained a process of data gathering, hypothesis formation leading to some action, followed by a review. As a result, the hypothesis could be adjusted and further action proposed. A series of working hypotheses could then be developed (which is a feature of action research methodology). In my practice I was confronted with children who caused concern for parents and educators, with resultant educational difficulties which needed to be resolved.

The contextual assessment approach contained four phases. These could be followed though not necessarily in any sequential order. The stages implied a degree of increased involvement or focusing by the assessor, whether that was myself or the parent, the teacher or an external professional.

The first stage involved an information gathering phase (see Figure 11.1). This involved receiving information and/or seeking information from all those involved with a child causing concern. The second phase of information gathering centred upon observations of the child-in-focus (see Figure 11.2). From my experience I was concerned that children appeared to play uneasily or less effectively in contexts which were unfamiliar to them. When I then compared these children's performances to those observed in their own homes, playgroups and/or nurseries, I realised that their demonstration of abilities through play in the natural setting gave more accurate information regarding a child's abilities in relation to the concerns raised in the teaching and learning context. According to Ysseldyke and Christenson (1987), when a child is assessed out of context, the information gained may have no bearing on the problems and difficulties which may be causing concerns in the teaching and learning context. This fact was also underlined in a DES (UK Department of Education and Science) circular (22/89 section 34) at that time.

Much of children's early play and language behaviours are ephemeral in nature. Therefore, the strategy of carrying out descriptive observations as the most effective form of recording children's play and language in context is a strong feature of the second phase in the developing assessment approach. There is a strong link here with qualitative research methodology, as I would argue that I was seeking to understand naturally occurring phenomena in their naturally occurring states.

There was an emphasis on the need for a collective perspective. My observations were always shared with the parents and educators in order to confirm interpretations and judgements. I shared my observations because I wanted to enrich my data by incorporating others' views, in order to develop a meaningful dialogue which would lead into the next phase of the assessment

Consultative approach		
Time	Referrals:	Information was often received in the form of referrals via parents, colleagues, schools, medical services.
	Parents:	Liaison with parents was important in order to learn as much as possible regarding the home background dynamics, the home learning context/environment, and a historical perspective of a concern.
	Other learning contexts/environments:	Obtaining perceptions from other adults in the other learning context/environments – i.e. Teachers/Supervisors/Nursery Nurses, was important to gain a wider perspective.
	Fellow professionals:	Liaison with other professionals involved – i.e. Speech Therapists, Occupational Therapists, Physiotherapists, Senior Clinical Medical Officers – in the form of reports plus personal contact. There was a valuing of other professional views/perceptions.
	Educational colleagues:	Discussions with colleagues enabled a sharing of ideas/perceptions, and the possibility of drawing upon their knowledge, expertise and experience.

Figure 11.1 Contextual approach to assessment: information gathering phase

process, e.g. planning a response to promote learning for a child-in-focus. So a second major principle in my thinking emerged through practice, relating to the need to share ideas and the range of multiple viewpoints in order to illuminate further understanding of a child's special educational needs.

The third phase (see Figure 11.3) I referred to as an experimentation phase, as I tested my hypotheses, and sought to influence the intervention strategies in the teaching and learning context in order to promote the learning of the child in question. I wanted also to improve the quality of learning experiences offered to children, within specific contexts as well as across settings.

In the UK, provision for children under five varies widely. Often this means that a child with possible special educational needs will attend a patchwork of provision, straddling any or all of the following sectors: Education (both mainstream and special school provision), Health, Social Services and Private providers. Whatever the nature of the provision or shared provision a child attended, the task remained the same: to observe, reflect and seek ways to improve the quality of learning and teaching.

Consultative approach		
Time	(a) Passive observations:	This phase contained the concept of continuous positive hypotheses formation. The educator is seen as an 'artist' not a 'technician' carrying out an assessment test. The observation process is aimed at trying to understand the child-in-focus's learning processes/abilities rather than isolated skills acquisition. As I observed I was seeking to identify patterns of behaviour, and to interpret what I perceived, in order to inform my advice and support for the parents and/or educators. The observational assessments take place in various natural environments and are therefore context specific (DES Circular 22/89 section 34). Examples of the qualities that I looked for in my observations are: • initiation of play • processing using all senses • focusing of attention • social cognition/interactive ability • communicative ability • emotional/social state • attitudes – motivation – perseverance • alertness – awareness In making judgements based upon the observations, I drew upon my training and past knowledge acquired about child development, and by comparing the child-in-focus with his/her peers. To interpret observational data from a child-in-focus in a segregated setting was less effective. Copies of observations were given to parents/educators as I encouraged feedback, in order to enhance the validity of the gathered data.
	(b) Interactive observations:	These type of observations tended to be play and language dominant. In these observation sessions I sought to understand how the child-in-focus created meaning from his/her experiences in the learning context/environment. The child-in-focus was allowed to create and shape the play and language dialogue. Examples of qualities I looked for in the interactive learning context/environment included: • responsiveness to intervention – play interaction – rapport development • potential for extension – intellectual extension – the creation of meaning • looking for structures of meaning – play processes at work – breadth of experiences • experimentation on my part – modelling – matching of activities to child's experience – relevancy notion • learning styles – approaches Results of interactive observations were always discussed with the parents and/or educators and any of the following points could have been considered: • pupil's individual learning style(s) and interests • appropriate teaching strategies • examination of methodological issues • consideration of class organisational factors • suggestion of appropriate curricula play activities • environmental issues.

Figure 11.2 Contextual approach to assessment: observation phase

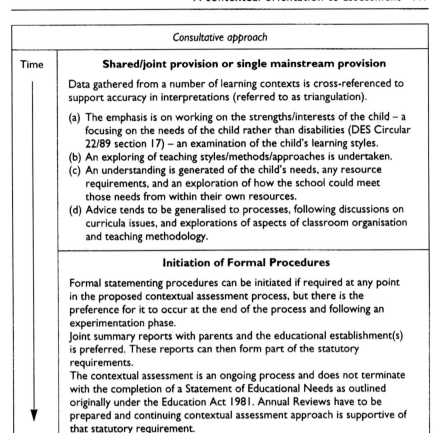

	Consultative approach
Time	**Shared/joint provision or single mainstream provision**
	Data gathered from a number of learning contexts is cross-referenced to support accuracy in interpretations (referred to as triangulation).
	(a) The emphasis is on working on the strengths/interests of the child – a focusing on the needs of the child rather than disabilities (DES Circular 22/89 section 17) – an examination of the child's learning styles.
	(b) An exploring of teaching styles/methods/approaches is undertaken.
	(c) An understanding is generated of the child's needs, any resource requirements, and an exploration of how the school could meet those needs from within their own resources.
	(d) Advice tends to be generalised to processes, following discussions on curricula issues, and explorations of aspects of classroom organisation and teaching methodology.
	Initiation of Formal Procedures
	Formal statementing procedures can be initiated if required at any point in the proposed contextual assessment process, but there is the preference for it to occur at the end of the process and following an experimentation phase.
	Joint summary reports with parents and the educational establishment(s) is preferred. These reports can then form part of the statutory requirements.
	The contextual assessment is an ongoing process and does not terminate with the completion of a Statement of Educational Needs as outlined originally under the Education Act 1981. Annual Reviews have to be prepared and continuing contextual assessment approach is supportive of that statutory requirement.

Figure 11.3 Contextual approach to assessment: formal assessment phase

It was through observing in a variety of contexts, that I began to see that the educational needs were not child specific, but also the educators and parents had needs which could affect the learning of a child. Educators may have needed help in understanding how children learn, how to organise the learning environment or marshal additional resources to promote learning opportunities, and/or how to plan and adjust their curriculum to meet the educational needs of particular children. Many parents I worked with had a variety of needs, particularly of an emotional character, as they came to terms with the difficulties their children were perhaps facing in their learning. They may have had needs in regard to knowledge about their rights and the formal assessment procedures that they were battling to understand and work through in relation to the UK Education Act 1981 (now 1996 Education Act). They may have needed support in actually teaching and helping their children through play and language in the home.

It was only through experimentation with teaching strategies, organisation of learning experiences, and/or adjusting resources, that I could develop as wide an understanding of the educational needs of a child as possible. In this phase, observations continued to take place in order to monitor the progress of a child-in-focus, as well as inform future dialogue, review and action.

By adopting a problem-solving approach to assessing the special educational needs, I discovered that some special educational needs were resolved, as the child was no longer a cause for concern in that specific teaching and learning context. I also discovered that some special educational needs were context related and once their needs were identified and supported, the child-in-focus no longer became a cause for concern.

However, there were situations where the child needed additional support and resources, and a decision to initiate formal assessment procedures under the UK Education Act 1981 resulted. I argued for this fourth phase (see Figure 11.3) to take place after a contextual assessment had occurred, as I believed that only then could the educational needs of the child-in-focus and the educator be ascertained. I felt that some decisions were made too soon, leading to children being segregated and denied the benefit and opportunity to interact and learn alongside their peers.

It may appear that I have produced a model of assessment, but I think that is to misunderstand the dynamic nature of this evolving orientation to assessment. One of the problems of describing an approach is to fix it in time, whereas in reality it is a dynamic process bound up with the socially interactive and reflective context of the teaching and learning interface where I work. I have attempted to articulate my thoughts and ideas. Through this process of articulation, I have not attempted to produce a model of assessment to be followed, but have sought to understand what the principles are that guide my practice.

Importance of differing viewpoints

A case study was compiled in order to clarify my thinking, to further elucidate the developing approach to assessment in relation to crystallising underlying principles. What came as a surprise were the limitations imposed upon my thinking by other colleagues from educational psychology and health agencies, who operated a different approach to assessment which did not value my perspective.

As a contextual orientation to assessment relies on, and actively seeks, a variety of perspectives concerning the special educational needs of pre-school children, it is not surprising that the possibility of a divergence of opinion is ever present between the various stakeholders in the assessment frame. Teaching and learning is a socially interactive process, which is context related. Social events such as teaching and learning need to be understood in terms of the perceptions or understandings of those involved, including the child, parents, educators and other professionals. The value of this possible divergence of opinion is that it can act educatively to alert one to aspects within the assessment process, and/or offer differing interpretations of data which one has not considered before (Bridges *et al*. 1986).

The term 'collectivity' is used to describe an important principle underpinning the development of a contextual orientation to assessment. The term comes from the word 'collective' which means to draw together many things, aspects, or ideas to form a compound or representative entity. In the assessment context I have used it to mean the drawing together of a range of perspectives or views of all those involved in the assessment of special education needs of pre-school children, to form a representative or collective viewpoint upon a child's learning needs. Translating this principle into practice is more problematical, as I discovered through the compilation of the case study.

The Rumbold Report (DES 1990), a UK Government document which outlines educational guidance for early-years practitioners, stresses the importance of gathering information on children's learning in a co-operative manner, involving health authorities and parents. The UK Code of Practice (DfEE 1994) states the importance of such collaborative practices (particularly in relation to special educational needs). The term 'collaborative' implies involvement and working together. It describes the development of positive working relationships between all those involved.

The implication of collaboration would seem to be the development of partnerships with colleagues. The Rumbold Report (DES 1990) states that partnership implies a two-way process, with knowledge and information flowing freely between people. The Report further states the need to exchange 'insights' between parties. Insights would seem to indicate more than just the exchange of information, there is an underlying assumption that it will have an effect on understanding. This would seem to imply that an information exchange may have an effect in increasing one's understanding, or illuminating the learning needs of the child-in-focus.

The aspect of sharing perspectives with others, or seeking alternative perspectives of others with differing knowledge and expertise, in order to enhance the illumination of understanding of a child's special educational needs, would seem to be more difficult to achieve than the more superficial level of collaboration.

Is it a question of who holds the power? An approach that does not value alternative perspectives, and is more positivist in orientation, is perhaps a dominant force in the field of special educational needs, and the judgements that result from such an approach act as powerful truth statements. If the parents are articulate and clear about how they see their child and what they want for their child, can their view dominate, even over those who operate a positivist orientated approach to assessment? If the parents are inarticulate, and unclear or hesitant about the learning needs of their child, can those who operate a positivist orientated approach to assessment prevail?

I am reminded of the work of Forest and Lusthaus (1989) on 'circles and maps'. In their work they argue for the establishment of a network of support (referred to as 'maps') offered to pupils to ensure successful integration into mainstream schools. The idea is that professionals and others (e.g. parents, children) join together to share their views and establish a common understanding of pupils' needs to ensure appropriate support is offered to pupils in mainstream settings. A strong feature of their work is the idea of collaboration and a collective approach to supporting pupils' learning. I would also advocate a similar notion in a contextual orientation to assessment, with professionals and parents working together to ensure appropriate support for a child's learning within a teaching and learning context. But can this work if colleagues are reluctant to share views and developing theories regarding the learning needs of children? Does successful sharing of perspectives rely upon professionals building up a network of contacts where trust prevails?

Forest and Lusthaus (1989) also describe the idea of a 'circle of friends'. I am reminded of the articulate parents of a child with cerebral palsy I worked with, who actively gathered around themselves a group of supporters, who came into their home to carry out a 'patterning' programme (a programme of regular and intensive physiotherapy) with their child. In addition, they sought out professionals who agreed with their view that their child was intelligent and should be educated in their local mainstream school. In the end, they had a circle of professionals who supported their perspective and enabled them to secure a mainstream context with appropriate support for their child, against a formidable array of sceptical professionals.

I am left questioning whether it is possible to operate a contextual orientation to assessment, with its emphasis on seeking alternative perspectives to develop a holistic and collective view of a child with special educational needs, when other approaches have a dominant positivist orientation and do not value a perspective other than their own? Perhaps, if the parents are articulate and know what they want, the power could shift from such dominant positivist orientated approaches to assessment. But are we in danger of establishing a new dominant perspective, which may be as biased or inaccurate as a statement emanating from a medically orientated model of assessment?

How does one know what is truth, or whether someone's perspective is accurate and true? In the positivist paradigm, truth statements are formed on objectively formed data, often resulting from some form of measurement. True interpretations of data gathered from the socially interactive context of the teaching and learning interface, in the interpretative paradigm, are dependent upon seeking a collective viewpoint, by the process of sharing and discussing various perspectives. The problem still remains as to how to distinguish between a false consensus and a true one? Carr and Kemmis (1986) discuss this issue in relation to the work of Habermas. They argue that the process of dialogue, as perspectives are shared, is the methodological process of seeking a collective view, which ensures against bias, prejudice and the misuse of power. The dialogue helps to test the truth claims of opinions, assuming that the participants in the dialogue are co-operating to search for truth. They argue that in a dialogue that is genuinely searching for truth, the interests of the participants will emerge, and the force of the argument or developing collective perspective will come to the fore. There needs to be a free flow of ideas and arguments, which is free from the threat of domination, manipulation and control by any one person or professional group.

Conclusion

The conclusion I draw from the exploration of this area of collectivity in practice, is that practices of collaboration can be achieved, but practices related to sharing perspectives are more problematical, constrained by people's orientation to assessment, time and a reluctance to share power. The frustrations caused as people with a contextual orientation to assessment encounter others who do not value a range of differing perspectives, is perhaps unavoidable. The theory of a contextual orientation to assessment would seem problematical to evolve in practice, and perhaps the concept of multiple perspectives is worthy of further empirical research.

The theory that emerged from my research is as follows:

> 'The assessment of special educational needs should be carried out in children's familiar teaching and learning contexts. It should encompass holistic data gathering practices. These include the early-years practices of carrying out of observations on children's learning, and sharing interpretations and developing theories regarding children's learning needs. Such an orientation to assessment, as illustrated by my developing contextual approach, should be able to be used in any child's familiar learning/teaching context. It will help educators to identify and meet the learning needs of a child causing concern, as well as identify what adjustments in the teaching context may be required to meet that child's special educational needs'.

I therefore argue that by adopting a contextual orientation to assessment a basis is provided for developing an assessment framework which will support educators in assessing the special educational needs of their pre-school children.

References

Bridges, D., Elliott, J. and Klass, C. (1986) 'Performance Appraisal as Naturalistic Inquiry: A Report of the Fourth Cambridge Conference on Educational Evaluation', *Cambridge Journal of Education* 16(3): 221–3.

Bronfenbrenner, U. (1979) *The Ecology of Human Development – Experiments by Nature and Design*, Cambridge MS: Harvard University Press.

Carr, W. and Kemmis, S. (1986) *Becoming Critical – Education, Knowledge and Action Research*, Lewes: The Falmer Press.

DES (1989) *Assessments and Statements of Special Educational Needs: Procedures within the Education, Health and Social Services*, Circular 22/89, London: Department of Education and Science

—— (1990) *Starting with Quality – The Rumbold Report*, London: Department of Education and Science.

DfEE (1994) *Code of Practice on the Identification & Assessment of Special Educational Needs*, London: Department for Education and Employment.

Elliott, J. (1976) *Developing Hypothesis about Classrooms from Teachers' Practical Constructs*, University of North Dakota Press.

Forest, M. and Lusthaus, E. (1989) 'Promoting Educational Equality for All Students Circles and Maps', in S. Stainback, W. Stainback, M. Forest, *Educating All Students in the Mainstream of Regular Education*, London: Paul Brookes.

Goodman, Y. (1978) 'Kid Watching: An Alternative to Testing', *National Elementary School Principal* **57**: 41–5.

Heshusius, L. (1991) 'Curriculum-Based Assessment and Direct Instruction: Critical Reflections on Fundamental Assumption', *Exceptional Children* **57**(4): 315–28.

Ysseldyke, J. and Christenson, S. (1987) 'Evaluating Students' Instructional Environments', *Remedial and Special Education* **8**(3): 17–24.

Chapter 12

Sheffield Early Childhood Association

A snapshot of Sheffield Practice

Sylvia Walker and Colleagues[1]

Introduction

This chapter aims to provide a snapshot of the growth of Sheffield Early Years Special Needs services. We have many dedicated people who have contributed to this chapter (see Acknowledgements at the end of this chapter) and I hope the particular individual snapshots may give others encouragement to develop similar programmes of Early Years and Special Needs.

All children have the need of inclusion through a well established, committed service and therefore in Sheffield we are able to present these Snapshots of Sheffield Practice within a number of 'Inclusion' perspectives. We look through the eyes of the members of Sheffield Early Childhood Association and share their experiences of working with special children and their families. These snapshots cover a wide and varied approach to special needs. (For background history to SECA see page 130.)

Inclusion 1

We will take steps through time starting with parents from the Pre-School Learning Alliance (PLA) and examples of providers working together in the public, private and voluntary sectors.

Inclusion 2

Bluestones Education Nursery and Norfolk Park Special School Inclusion Team.

Inclusion 3

Moving on to a private nursery provider and a parent's comments and linking the practice.

---

[1] See Acknowledgements at the end of this chapter.

Inclusion 4

Sheffield Young Children's Centre covers a wide range of support to families and works as a co-operative. One of the unique aspects of the centre is its staffing – 50 per cent male, 50 per cent female.

Inclusion 5

Support Teaching and Education Psychology Service (STEPS).

The chapter then goes on to provide a brief history of Sheffield Early Child-hood Association and a description of Sheffield Young Children's Service with details of Early Years Training in Special Educational Needs.

Inclusion 1: PLA snapshots of practice – voluntary and private sector working together

The Sheffield branch of the Pre-School Learning Alliance is fully committed to enabling children with a very wide variety of extra support needs into its groups. In the last decade the demand for specialist support has led the Management Committee to put in various bids to charitable causes in order to provide support workers in playgroups, pre-schools and parent and toddler groups.

The two main ways we have provided support have been through (i) specific projects; and (ii) an extensive special needs training programme. Specific projects have included an 'Opportunities for Volunteering Integration Project' and at present the 'Pre-School Inclusion Project'. Through both of these projects many children in Sheffield have been able to attend mainstream groups. These groups have also given support to parents experiencing the pressures associated with the statementing procedure.

What do our clients, families and pre-schools (playgroups) have to say about the scheme?

All schemes require feedback and monitoring of results. Parents of client children and pre-school (playgroup) staff were asked to complete a questionnaire about whether the scheme had been useful or not. This is what the parents had to say:

> This scheme gave my child a start in life. We wanted him to go to main-stream nursery if possible. The Integrated Scheme proved to us that he could hold down a place at mainstream nursery with assistance. He has now started mainstream nursery with an assistant in much the same way as he had an assistant at playgroup.

> I think it is an excellent scheme giving support and encouragement to the child, parent and playgroup leaders. It enables children with Special Needs from an early age to integrate fully with other children from this community.

Pre-School (playgroup) leaders were asked, 'Has having a child with special needs in your pre-school (playgroup) been of value to the children and/or staff? This is what they had to say:

> It has certainly been of value
> a) to the staff, who came to realise how easy integration could be with individual support for a child with special needs;
> b) to the children who learn to accept others as they are.

> The playgroup children have accepted the child from the beginning. They appear to be aware he is different but do not distance themselves from him. I think having him at playgroup makes them aware that not all children are the same.

In answer to the question 'How has the child benefited?', we received the following opinions:

> He is able to mix with other children and takes part in all the playgroup activities:- painting, cookery, jigsaws, bike riding, etc. We have been able to take a child with special needs which we could not otherwise have done.

General comments:

> The project is an excellent idea, and helps playgroups to provide for children with special needs within their local area.

Lastly, a comment from one of our co-ordinators:

> The scheme has demonstrated that there is a very great need in the community for support for pre-school children with special needs in playgroups.

At the moment 12 children are being supported in pre-schools city wide and further referrals are constantly being made. In order to enable this work to take place, Sheffield PLA has worked in partnership with Sheffield Young Children's Service to promote a Special Needs Integrated Project training programme known as the 'Educare Project'. This is funded by European money and an extensive special needs training programme has been delivered to people living, working or working with children from 'Priority 5' areas of the city (areas of social disadvantage).

During the last 3 years more than 400 people have accessed this training and approximately 40 of these have been employed to support children with special needs in a variety of childcare settings.

Below are statements made by supervisors of groups who have employed Educare trained staff with help from the Young Children's Service Special Needs Support budget.

1   'This support has been invaluable to Playgroup, to the child's mum and particularly for the child. She has been able to be part of Playgroup, joining in with us all, and we believe everyone has benefited.'

2   'Thank you so much for the cheque to provide support for Child 1. But more than that, thank you for caring enough to organise this support both for Child 1 and for Child 2. I can't tell you how much this has meant to both families. Child 1 is really progressing now and is becoming more and more responsive and Child 2 is already starting to say a few single words out loud, he finds NO particularly useful!

Both parents have asked me to pass on their thanks to you and your team. Do pop in and see us if you are in the area.'

(Names deleted for confidentiality reasons)

These are just a few of the many responses we have received, reflecting the value of the work the Pre-School Learning Alliance in Sheffield has been doing in order to promote integrated child care in under-fives provision. We hope to continue and expand this area of work in the next millennium.

Inclusion 2: Positive experiences of interaction between a nursery class and a special school

Our experience from Bluestones Nursery (LEA) Staff

We work in a 39-place nursery in an inner city area with two teachers and two nursery nurses.

In September 1995 we were visited by two staff from the Special School near to our nursery. They wanted to start a playgroup once a week for their own pupils and other pre-school children. I saw this as an opportunity for our children to interact with children who they might see as 'strange' and to help them overcome feelings of fear about children in wheelchairs, or with obvious disabilities. When I asked parents if they approved of the visits most thought it was a very good idea and some asked if they could also come. The Special School could send a minibus to collect us and we agreed that one member of staff would take the older group of children – eight each time – and stay with them. A parent would help in the nursery to offset the loss of a staff member.

So every Tuesday morning we had a journey in a minibus to the Special School to play with some friends. When entering the Special School the most noticeable aspect was the silence – no children noises, no bustling around. It was interesting walking past all the high chairs and different aids the children sat and stood in to eat dinner. Initially we went into a classroom where we found similar play provision to Nursery and we all sat down together for a snack. Our friends used feeder cups and we drank from mugs.

After our snack we would go into the hall or play in the large ball pool and on other physical play equipment – we loved this. We met Paul who was blind and we sang songs for him, helped him play with sound pipes and crinkly paper – back at Nursery we kept our eyes closed and tried to move around the nursery. We met Linsay who had just 1 finger instead of a hand and who was learning to walk – but she could laugh and smile. Adam screamed a lot and pulled our hair – someone was frightened of him but most could cope with him.

Gradually, over time, some of the children came to visit our Nursery. Richard was very boisterous and clumsy but loved to say our names – he began to recognise some of our children and they were pleased to play with him in our Nursery. When we had visiting children from Special School several nursery children were especially pleased to see our friends and wanted to play with them.

We continued to visit Norfolk Park School until floods damaged the room last year. Although we haven't visited the school, the Norfolk Park staff have brought the children to nursery to play with us. We love them to come and our children always rush to say hello – they tend to accept them, watch them, then just play with them. It helps that there is always one member of staff for each visiting child. They are free to move around the nursery and play with anything on offer.

Children have attended the nursery on a regular basis prior to entering mainstream school, parents and children have been on an outing with us, we have borrowed leg braces and walking frames for our children to 'try out' and continue to welcome our special friends whenever they can manage to come to see us.

The room has been cleaned up since the floods and we have now re-established our visits (March 1999). The children from Norfolk Park School have continued to visit our nursery.

As an adult, working with boisterous but healthy children, I was very apprehensive about how I would cope seeing children with severe disabilities. I have found it a relief to know I can easily talk to and touch these children and smile at them and sing to them. In fact, it has made it easier for me to smile in a natural way and sometimes converse with disabled adults in wheelchairs in the streets and shopping malls.

Our experience from the Norfolk Park School Inclusion Team

Norfolk Park School is a school in Sheffield, which caters for children with severe and complex learning difficulties, aged between 2½ and 11 years. The NPS Inclusion Team is responsible for providing access to mainstream peers for as many of our children as possible. To enable us to do this, we have made various links with local schools where whole classes join together and share topics, social events, resources etc. This has proved to be very successful and we now have links for our nursery, infant and junior units with three different local schools. We also take individual children to their local school for 1–2 sessions per week to work alongside their peers.

We have found, through experience, that this is beneficial for all children involved. Our children benefit greatly, as it provides role models for acceptable behaviour and offers the opportunity for them to communicate with their peers. It also enables our children to interact with their peers, developing their social awareness, personal skills and offers the chance to develop friendships with children without disabilities, leading to opportunities to be included into the wider community.

Teachers in the mainstream schools have often been very surprised how much their children benefit from the experience. They tell us that their children develop positive attitudes and more realistic views towards others who are different from themselves. They say it also helps to abate the fear of disabilities, which is usually borne from a lack of knowledge. Their children also become more caring and develop a sense of acceptance and responsibility for those less able in our society. There is also a greater sense of sharing and co-operation between all children. Most of all, it provides models of individuals who may successfully achieve despite challenges. We often find that it is the children with many problems of their own who are drawn to our children. They have often experienced for themselves what it feels like to be different, how difficult it is to struggle with learning or even how tough life can really be. Befriending our children often gives them a sense of purpose and a feeling, sometimes for the first time, that they can be of such benefit to someone else. This in turn boosts their self esteem greatly, thus proving the whole experience can be so mutually beneficial.

We often find teachers who are very sceptical about having children with severe or complex learning difficulties in their classroom. They find the idea frightening, or wonder what benefit there would be for their children. All we can say to these teachers is – be open-minded, give it a go, you will probably be very surprised at the positive effect it does have on all children – and adults – concerned.

Inclusion 3: Woodhouse Nursery – private sector

Bryony is a delightful member of the nursery and like every other child can be mischievous at times and very independent. She settled in well, adjusted to a different routine when she celebrated her second birthday and moved into a larger and probably more noisy room.

Her records show she is progressing well in all aspects of development, especially her linguistic/comprehension skills. Nothing spectacular in that you may say – but Bryony is profoundly deaf.

Bryony's parents came to visit and see the nursery operating and ask if it would be a problem to take Bryony for 3 days (from 9.00 to 3.30). The peripatetic teacher who had been working closely with the family would visit weekly (and continues to do so) for approximately 1 hour – giving advice and discussing the activities and maybe designing a programme to work to. Various videos are taken to monitor her progress.

The staff and owners were involved in discussion with the teacher as to how Bryony might benefit from the nursery setting. I had completed a module on hearing impairment as part of a special needs course on integration. The course was organised by the Local Authority and accredited by the Open College Network. The course certainly came in useful to help Bryony.

The staff have been taught how to replace hearing aids if pulled out and continue the programme set out by Jane, the teacher, within the nursery environment. It is hoped that after extensive testing for both Bryony and her parents a cochlear implant will be possible. If it is not, the staff will be more than willing to learn sign although at the moment this is not necessary and Bryony will continue her education at her local school.

Thankfully it may be a while before a change is made so we continue to enjoy and observe Bryony's progress and especially that special smile and a welcome 'Hiya' or a wave and a 'Bye'.

Bryony's parents' comments from a review of Bryony's progress (March 1999) were: 'We are very well satisfied with all aspects of her progress. She is beginning to say more words and we are very pleased with her progress with the peripatetic teacher.'

Inclusion 4: Sheffield Children's Centre – community sector

Sheffield Children's Centre is an award winning comprehensive, childcare, education, play, training and family support service catering for children from birth to 18 years. The Centre is a co-operative for the benefit of the community and has been operational for 16 years. The Centre has always had inclusive policies and practices based upon equal rights. As a consequence 50 per cent male and 50 per cent female staff are employed; currently 80 per cent of the multi-disciplinary staff are from black and other minority ethnic communities and several staff have disabilities. The Centre is managed by service users (children and adults), local community representatives and workers.

The egalitarian nature of the provision ensures that a wide range of services are delivered to children, young people and their families who have special needs.

For inclusive early-years provision these include:

- linked childminding services
- before, after school and holidays provisions
- children with special needs, self help groups
- parent support groups
- advocacy services
- welfare rights and legal advice specific to children and their families
- culturally specific support groups
- respite provision
- additional support services

- counselling services
- facilitating holidays for families where a child or young person has special needs
- information base
- toy library

The Centre works in a multi-agency way to ensure early identification and assessment and appropriate service delivery. It also delivers and supports provisions for children with special needs world wide, therefore reaching a number of multi-ethnic communities.

The Centre is currently developing The Shack, an International Centre for Children's Arts and Culture to be based in Sheffield. This is being developed by children and young people themselves via a Children's Council. Children with special needs are substantially represented on the Children's Council.

Sheffield Children's Centre firmly believes that childhood is a status in its own right and should be valued and that children with special needs should not be on the margins of society or childhood culture but included in it as a right.

Inclusion 5: Support, Teaching and Education Psychology Service (STEPS)

Because of the unique aspect of child care in Sheffield there is a strong lead taken by the Support, Teaching and Educational Psychology Service (STEPS) which forms part of the Sheffield Education Service. Sheffield's inclusion policy and support for children with special needs is a priority within the Service.

Two of the development targets of the Sheffield Behaviour Support Plan 1999/2001 are:

- to give effective support, including early intervention and preventative measures, to schools, early-years providers and families provided through co-ordinated, multi-agency working
- to offer a comprehensive range of training and professional development opportunities to support schools and early-years providers in both encouraging positive behaviour and managing difficult behaviour. The quality of provision is monitored

A brief history of Sheffield Early Childhood Association

The Sheffield Early Childhood Association is an organisation, the history of which dates back to the very beginnings of Nursery Education in Sheffield. The Nursery Schools Association was founded in 1928 following the opening of Denby Street Nursery School. The National Nursery Schools Association changed its name in the early 1970s to the British Association for Early Childhood Education.

In the early 1980s, the Sheffield group decided to secede from the National Association and SECA was formed.

SECA has for many years broadened its membership from a strong foundation of Sheffield Nursery Schools to embracing the public, voluntary and private sector colleagues. The areas of special needs and young children have often been a focus for seminars and meetings. In Sheffield we have built very good early-years foundations and good practice, therefore the opportunity to celebrate and share these experiences will be especially valuable as we approach the millennium. Communication is one of the key factors in inclusion of all children and within Sheffield we now have the Young Children's Service which was established in 1994 and is part of Sheffield Education Service.

The aims of the Sheffield Early Childhood Association are:

- to form links between those working with young children in different parts of the city, from different departments of the local authority and the voluntary sector
- to disseminate information and promote discussion about early childhood issues
- to represent the concerns of those working with young children and their families, and, if necessary, act as a pressure group

Over the past 15 years we have had monthly meetings and held our annual conferences. The programme of meetings is drawn up by the Committee from topics suggested by members. One of the most successful seminars was on special needs and early years.

Sheffield Young Children's Service within the LEA

Role and structure

Sheffield Young Children's Service was set up as an integrated service within the Education Department (bringing together services from both social services and education) in Sheffield in 1994, with a remit to:

- develop and lead a city-wide strategy for the expansion of services for young children
- develop and lead a partnership approach
- develop universal quality
- co-ordinate training and development
- promote an inclusive service

The Service is responsible, under the Children Act 1989, for the registration and inspection of private and voluntary sector early-years services in the city. It is also a provider of direct services: of six nursery schools and seven young children's centres.

The Government has recently given the LEA/Young Children's Service greater responsibility for planning and expanding early-years services, in partnership with the Sheffield Early Years Development Partnership. The Young Children's Service, with the Partnership, produces the Early Years Development and Childcare Plan and will in future also be responsible for developing the childcare strategy.

The new childcare strategy, recently announced by the Government, will give additional responsibilities to the Young Children's Service, and to the Early Years Development Partnership to expand and deliver integrated early education and childcare, with a remit for children from babies up to the age of 14 years. The Government wants to see:

- better outcomes for children, including readiness to learn by the time they reach school and enjoyable, developmental activities out of school hours; and
- more parents with the chance to take up work, education or training because they have access to diverse, good quality childcare. (See Chapter 1).

Access to services

- YCS provides support within its direct services for children and families.
- Many of the direct services in partnership with other organisations provide a variety of additional services to support children and families.
- The service works closely with the STEPS team.
- External funding facilitates additional support for children with special needs.

Current developments

- YCS with the Early Years Development Partnership aims to expand family and support services.
- It aims to appoint a Parent Partnership Co-ordinator and to develop a parent led 'Parents Forum'.
- It aims to develop multi-agency partnerships.
- The YCS aims to develop and promote the Childcare Strategy that was sent to the DfEE in January 1999, which involved the Early Years Development Partnership and would ensure good quality affordable childcare to children aged 0–14 years in every neighbourhood.

Snapshots of Special Needs within the Sheffield Young Children's Service

Sheffield City Council is committed to quality services for all young children. Equality, quality and partnership are central to every aspect of planning for the future.

The foundation for working together in Sheffield is its area planning structure. This process brings together all providers and all with an interest in early years on a *local* basis. It aims to represent a picture of local needs, gaps and opportunities and to allow for opportunities for local collaboration and partnership. It is also the route for accessing views of parents area by area.

Sheffield Early Years Development Partnership consists of three constituent parts:

- **The Development Partnership** – this brings together representatives of the different interests in early years on a city-wide basis.
- **The Development Partnership Seminars** – the seminars bring together up to three representatives from each of the area planning groups with the Development Partnership Group.
- **The Development Partnership Task Groups** – each Task Group will be represented on the Development Partnership Group and will make recommendations to the Group on specific areas of work.

The Early Years SEN Task Group has been established by the Early Years Development Childcare Partnership with a broad representative membership. Its brief is to:

- translate the Partnership's general aims relevant to Special Educational Needs (SEN) into an implementation plan
- monitor the plan, and
- report back to the Early Years Development Childcare Partnership and other relevant Task Groups

The Early-Years SEN Task Group will establish policy proposals for the Development Partnership building upon the key policy objectives of the City Council in relation to Early Years.

The Task Group will propose a plan with clear development targets which will be linked to other relevant plans and activities including:

- The Children's Services Plan
- The Education Development Plan
- The City Achievement Strategy
- The Child and Adolescent Mental Health Strategy
- The Behaviour Support Plan
- Multi-agency and parent partnership working groups
- The LEA's Special Educational Needs Policy

Inclusion

The LEA in partnership with the Task Group plans to help mainstream providers increase their abilities to provide for a wide range of children's needs. Given the existing levels of expertise, not all parents wish to opt for mainstream provision and special provision will continue to be an integral part of our range.

Quality of provision

To improve the quality of provision it is necessary to listen to the views of parents and involve them in decisions about services, individually and collectively.

The Young Children's Service has run a City-wide quality programme 'Starting Together'. It is now running the second phase, 'Developing Together', which is developing a 'Quality Kite Mark' to complement existing inspection frameworks, setting specific frameworks for self-evaluation. The Early-Years Special Needs Task Group will have a representative on the Quality Task Group and will be fully involved in this work.

Prevention and early intervention

Intervention needs to be early if we are to ensure children and families benefit. There are a number of models of good practice that have been developed for early assessment. These have continued to improve the co-ordination of health professionals, social services and education staff to ensure that the majority of children with severe special needs are identified early and well before they are of statutory school age. There is, however, a common view that an emphasis upon increasing the co-ordination and range of provision for early intervention is crucial.

Programmes of early intervention involving home visiting, such as that provided by the LEA's Portage Service, clearly demonstrate that families can be the most effective and economical system for fostering and sustaining the development of young children with special needs. Programmes supporting early inclusion into local community pre-schools and parent and toddler groups (such as the Pre-School Learning Alliance project which supports parents and voluntary community groups and works with statutory support services to achieve successful integration for children and families at an early stage) need to be supported. Preventive strategies and early intervention programmes should be provided within a context of family support.

Sheffield LEA operates a city-wide scheme of baseline assessment for all children when they begin primary education. The LEA, with the Task Group, will consider how best to utilise this scheme, as part of the City's Achievement Strategy, to target preventative strategies and early intervention to where needs are identified – whether these arise from special educational needs, from family or emotional difficulties.

Multi-agency approach

The Code of Practice for the identification and assessment of Special Educational Needs provides a framework for all agencies and providers to have a multi-agency approach. When concerns are felt about the progress of a child, parents and professionals need to have a clear understanding of when, where and how to involve services and how they co-ordinate together. All of the services need to clarify what resources they contribute to family support and early intervention in relation to the *Code of Practice*.

In line with the policies of the City Council it is an expectation that, unless there are compelling reasons why not, all children will be provided for through mainstream education and care provision.

Currently:

- The Local Authority, including the Young Children's Service, working with other agencies will provide training, advice and guidance to all providers, including private and voluntary agencies, concerning the Code of Practice.
- All providers are capable, with support where necessary from the SEN Support Service, of identifying and assessing special needs.
- The criteria for the assessment of pre-school SEN and access to additional support has been reviewed. Revised criteria will be established within the year.
- All providers will be supported by a range of staff development opportunities and, where concerns are felt about individual children, from the range of statutory agencies support services.
- The SEN Support Service involves a range of teaching and educational psychology support. It provides an under 5s team with close links to Health and Family and Community Services in providing advice to parents and all providers.
- The SEN Support Service also provides a Portage home-visiting service to families of children with severe special needs and the LEA will seek to increase the size of this service as soon as resources allow.
- SUMES (Sheffield Unified Multi-cultural Education Service) provides direct support to early-years children with special needs who require support for English as an additional language.
- Sheffield Advisory and Inspection Service, Education Training and Development Section, together with managers from the Young Children's Service can provide support for training, management and evaluation for all providers.

Sheffield can be justly proud of these achievements and of the range and quality of its special needs Early-Years provision. There is much, however, that can and should be done to continue to improve.

Acknowledgements

Contributors to this chapter are:

- Sylvia Walker, SECA Co-ordinator and Principal Training and Development Officer, Sheffield LEA, Personnel Services

- Jill Shaw, Early-Years Special Needs Co-ordinator, Sheffield Young Children's Service
- Sheffield Early Childhood Association – Committee Members
- Members of Pre-School Learning Alliance
- Sheffield Young Children's Service
- STEPS – Support Teaching and Educational Psychology Service
- Pauline Zelaieta and June Godbert – Norfolk Park Inclusion Team
- Clare Sandercock – Bluestone Nursery
- Chrissy Maleady – Sheffield Children's Centre
- Margaret Carr – Woodhouse Nursery

A special thank you to Kathy Lewis for the secretarial support of this chapter.

Appendix: early-years training for Special Educational Needs

There is a steady increase in the provision of courses/development opportunities for all those who work with children with Special Educational Needs. Some of these are listed below:

- Sheffield Young Children's Service organise and deliver courses on Special Needs funded through 'Educare' (European Social Fund). These are targetted to those working in priority areas of the city. Reference to this funding is highlighted in the PLA snapshot (Inclusion 1).
- The PLA deliver workshops with specific special needs elements.
- The Sheffield Portage Scheme organises and delivers training courses. This is part of STEPS.
- The Sheffield College deliver courses that have special needs elements, for example:

    Advanced Diploma in Child Care and Education
    Diploma in Nursery Nursing
    Play Therapy
    Open College Accredited Course on National Vocational Qualification underpinning knowledge. Level 2/3 Childcare and Education.

- The Sheffield Early-Years Assessment Centre consists of partnership between Sheffield LEA, The Sheffield College and the voluntary and private sector. The centre attracts Further Education funding and has 250 candidates registered on NVQ Level 2/3 Childcare and Education. Many NVQ Level 3 candidates have completed the Units for Special Needs. A SEYAC candidate was nominated for a Silver Medal for Excellence award by City and Guilds. She was awarded the medal in May 1998. The silver medal is the highest level awarded at NVQ Level 3.

- The Sheffield Education Service Training & Development Section organise:
  - Induction Courses for Child Care Assistants who work with statemented children. 280 received training in 1998.
  - Behavioural Support programmes tutored by Behaviour Support Teachers. 300 places on courses 1998/99.
  - Open College Courses for Child Care Assistants who work with children with Special Educational Needs – tutored by Educational Psychologists. 40 staff per year attend.
  - Partnership links are taking place with Barnsley LEA. They have a Credit Accumulated Transfer Scheme accredited programme for their Special Needs Assistants. We will be looking at using their programme/materials in the near future.
  - Nursery Nurses and Child Care Assistants have courses specifically designed for Special Needs, e.g. Hearing Impairment, Communication Skills.
  - Special Needs Diploma at Hallam University CATS accredited.
  - Asthma Care courses delivered by the Sheffield Children's Hospital and Northern General Hospital Respiratory Nurses.

Because of recent developments and legislation child care has at last hit the headlines and therefore there is more flexibility to how training is delivered and access to qualifications other than the college or University routes. We need to hold on to Sheffield's many good quality child care initiatives and the varied training programmes that are offered to staff, parents and volunteers.

Index

Printed in the United Kingdom
by Lightning Source UK Ltd.
135667UK00001B/37/A